WOMEN LIKE ME

Transforming Pain into Wisdom and Love

Compiled by Julie Fairhurst

WOMAN LIKE ME

TRANSFORMING PAIN INTO WISDOM AND LOVE

JULIE FAIRHURST

CONTENTS

"A dove struggling in a storm grows stronger than an eagle soaring in sunshine."
Matshona Dhliwayo

INTRODUCTION

WOMAN LIKE ME: TRANSFORMING PAIN INTO WISDOM AND LOVE

Life has a way of throwing challenges at us, often when we least expect them. It's in these moments of struggle and pain that we discover our true strength, our resilience, and the deep well of wisdom that resides within us.

This book, Woman Like Me: Transforming Pain into Wisdom and Love, is a testament to the incredible journey of eleven women who faced their hardships head-on and emerged stronger, wiser, and more loving.

Each story in this collection is a beacon of hope, a reminder that no matter how difficult the journey, there is always a path to healing and growth. These women, from diverse backgrounds and walks of life, have opened their hearts to share their experiences with you. They have faced loss, betrayal, illness, and adversity, yet they have found ways to transform their pain into something beautiful and meaningful.

Their stories are not just about the challenges they encountered but about the remarkable transformations that took place within them. Through their stories, you will see how they navigated their darkest moments, found healing in unexpected places, and learned to embrace love and wisdom even in the face of suffering.

This book celebrates the human spirit and the power of community. It shows how we can find strength and inspiration by sharing our stories and supporting each other. The women in these pages are not just survivors; they are thrivers. They have turned their pain into a power source and used their experiences to help others heal and grow.

As you read Woman Like Me: Transforming Pain into Wisdom and Love, you will be inspired by the courage and resilience of these incredible women. Their stories will remind you that you are not alone in your struggles and that there is always a way to find light in the darkness.

Let their journeys be a source of strength and a guide to transforming your own pain into wisdom and love.

Julie Fairhurst

Founder of Women Like Me

"Don't fear pain and do not run from it but allow it to transform you to the person you were created to be."
Nontobeko Jobe

PART 1

WOMEN LIKE ME

TRANSFORMING PAIN INTO WISDOM
AND LOVE

I WILL WAIT: CREATE YOUR OWN UNIQUE VISION TO EMERGE AS A QUEEN

LOIS A UNGER

"Allow the light within to shine."
Shakti Gawain

Have you ever convinced yourself "I will wait" until...

- I have longer hair.
- I have more education.
- My body shape is perfect.
- Someone invites me.
- I have the right car or house and many other lines.

And then missed out on a lot of great opportunities because of the statements you have repeated to yourself. This self-sabotage mindset leads to a familiar daily life and hopes that one day, you will reclaim the life you desire.

For many years, I was afraid to step out of my comfort zone. I knew I had more potential but was afraid to ask for what I wanted and needed. I would repeat harsh statements to myself over and over again every single day from the time I woke up. "I'm not good enough, I'm too busy, I can't do that, I won't answer the phone, I can't attend, I don't have time, I don't have anything to wear."

Even though, secretly, I wanted to be out there and enjoy life more. These statements and many others consumed me daily for years. YEARS!!!! How is that? Why didn't I change? What was stopping me? Did I like the familiarity on a daily basis? Was it easier to just let life pass by? Will I die alone?

I was very independent and mature from a young age. I am the youngest of seven, and I grew up on a small hobby farm. Every day after school, I would have chores to do before supper: gardening, hauling in drinking water from the well, mowing the lawn, feeding animals, cleaning the kitchen, and doing school homework. In the evenings, my mom and I would share a grapefruit and play a game, or my dad would play the harmonica or accordion, and we would sing. Life was simple and rewarding.

After mom died in a horrific car accident and dad a few years later left me to step out of my comfort zone as this was about midlife for me. I learned that growth happens when I push beyond my limits, set healthy boundaries, realize my full potential, and don't just dream about your vision board. Make it a reality and say YES!!

I found my missing pieces to my life as I bridged the gaps. I had plenty of aspirations and intentions, and finally, I could clearly see how to rewire my life story and inner dialogue.

I learned to change my mindset, fire up neurons, and create new patterns. I began to be a risk taker, reflecting daily on my life with meditation, reading positive notes, and using I am affirmations.

I embraced the changes of the new me. I seized moments, became relentless in my livelihood, and let my radiance show through. I emerged like a force, reclaimed my beautiful inner self, and I am so grateful daily. I took action, and the universe delivered.

At one point, it seemed like I had two lives: the one I was just living and not participating in and the one I envisioned in my mind. Today, I am grateful I let the flame glow and eventually set it on fire.

Do you know we have over 60,000 thoughts a day? 60,000!!!!!!. 90 % of our thoughts are repetitive, and 75% are negative. I find this fascinating. Our three-pound brain can process this. According to Google, most of the brain's neurons are already created at birth. However, we are also able to stimulate new neural growth.

Exercise-body movement, nutrient-dense food choices, rest, being socially involved, reading, music, and doing something different daily. Our cognitive peak is about age 35 and declines after age 45.

This is when I created a new behavior and did not let any barriers be in my way. I created confidence as we are not born with it. I embraced a new lifestyle.

Action is the key to a fulfilled life. There is nothing to fear except our thoughts holding us back. Draw up a new plan and make waves.

When I reflect on my life, I am grateful for my wellness and how I have surpassed my goals. I owned a camera from a young age, and I was intrigued by photography and the stories a picture holds. Today, I have several cameras and love taking pictures because they are pure bliss and enjoyment.

Driving in the country and being surrounded by nature, hearing the birds, seeing the crops bloom, watching a sunrise shimmer on an old church-stained glass window. I call myself a photo artist and print my images on several different items as shops will happily display them. Art shows are another great way to meet fellow creatives and share skills.

These are experiences that elevate my life.

The love of the arts also led me to sign up as a model. This has been life-changing and enriching my life and my health on all levels. Many times, I am assured that there is room for everyone in this world—no matter who you are.

I have been selected as a runway fashion model for fundraisers and women's trade shows, brand photoshoots, films, ads, commercials, and videos, published in print magazines, canoed on the river, quad in a field, lunch in a five-star restaurant, and acted as a client checking in a popular hotel, wiener roast on a winter day, hiking, snowshoeing, and signing up as a product ambassador.

This is how I have been able to impact lives and rebuild my own. I'm so glad I hold space for all the various opportunities.

Modeling has become a release for me, and I let my curiosity lead the way. There are so many facets to this gift of work.

Just recently, I was a guest on a podcast, and many new facts of my life were revealed. In the end, I felt like a burden was lifted off of me because I had been ashamed of some of these moments.

If you ask yourself, "I could never do that," why would they choose me?"

Change your mindset and believe you can. Choose your passion. What do you love to do? What lights you up? What keeps you up at night? What can you not stop thinking about?

Do that!!!!!

Do that for yourself! Put yourself first. Get clear on what you want, believe you want it, and receive it with gratitude. Then, take action and see your happy face light up.

"The gift of life, gives you the greatest opportunity to live and chance to rise above any situation. With hopeful attitude you can overcome any struggle."

Lailah Gifty Akita

2

EMBRACING MY WISE WOMAN: MY PATH TO SPIRITUAL SEEKING

TERRI-LYNNE CATHERINE

"The only constant in life is change."
Heraclitus

For as long as I can remember. I have been a Seeker, a searcher of who and why we exist. I first experienced something "other" when I was five and a half years old. It was after I experienced some heavy trauma when three boys dragged me to the railroad tracks up in Castlegar, British Columbia, where we lived, and filled my panties with those sharp rocks while holding me down.

When I came home, I was terrified, and so was my mom. She told me not to ever tell my Dad, and if I did, she would say I was lying!

I became feverish with tonsilitis, which seems fitting now as I could not speak my truth. Before I went to the hospital and had my tonsils and adenoids removed, I was leaving my body in a feverish state, and I actually climbed the wall. My Mom said she would have to pull me down from the headboard.

It was a strange time. I remember I was trying to get to who I now understand as my guide. I'm unsure if I knew who or what he was. He was just an old man with a long white beard and long white hair in a long white robe, and he made me feel safe when my life around me wasn't always safe.

It's like a painting in my mind: me sitting on his lap and him holding me and just thinking about him takes me right back to the feeling of safety, warmth, and love. Some people may call him God. Maybe he is, but to me, he's my guide. He is magic. He's my safe place. I call him Merlin now.

When we moved back to Burnaby in 1968, I went to Sunday school in a good Baptist Church. I loved the feeling there. There seemed to be a spirit of love in that Church and all the children, especially my first Teacher, who was an amazing young woman.

She taught us about the kind and loving Jesus. Again, I felt safe in my life at that time. Until I was seven when one of my cousins taught us to play strip poker. He was probably 15 at the time, and we always lost. I think this was another trauma for me as I knew this was another "bad" thing I was part of.

My mom was Mennonite, and this is where the Anabaptist fore and brimstone teachings came from. She wasn't living as a Mennonite anymore but was brought up that way in

Saskatchewan during the dirty thirties; it was ingrained in my poor Mom and all her siblings.

We went to Sunday school for several years until I was too old to go; we were now living in Langley, where we moved to in 1972 when I was ten years old. When I had to join the adults in church part, it became a totally different feeling for me. It didn't feel safe, and it didn't feel right. I missed Sunday school, and I missed my teachers. After a while, Mom let us stay home on Sundays, and we no longer had to go. But as a young child of 12. I was still a Seeker like I've always been.

I started watching Evangelical sermons on Sundays. At that time, it was black-and-white TV, and we only had two channels that worked. The man's name was Rex Humbard, and I faithfully watched him every Sunday. I gave $1.00 of my $2.00 allowance each week to his ministry; I was a dedicated soul.

Alas, Rex was an adulterer. He fooled around on his wife and lost his ministry to Pat Boone. I was devastated. I can't even tell you how devastated I was that this man would do that to his wife, who I thought was wonderful.

I wrote a letter in complete horror and indignation and received a personalized letter from Pat Boone himself, asking me to forgive Rex and to not give up on the church or the ministry and that they were moving forward under his guidance. But after that, it was never the same for me, and I turned my back on the church. Without really realizing this was what I had done.

I remember being introduced to alcohol and pot at that time, and I was not a good drinker—never have been. I got myself into some trouble over the years. By age 17, I was friends with some people who were studying Wicca. My best friend Rick got me to read Lord of the Rings. He said the whole series was a good place to start on your spirit journey, and you know what? It was!

It taught me about good and evil in a different kind of way than the Church teaches. It taught about magic and the ability of the little person to overcome great strife and succeed in life. It's a magical series. I love it. (Then there is also Gandalf!) And so my spirit journey began in earnest.

Now, over the years. I was what you would call a true wild woman. I lived life to the fullest. By the time I was in my late 20s, I was in some trouble. And I needed to change my path. I went into rehab for the first time and had my 29th birthday there. I found my spirituality all over again.

But again, it leaned into faith-based Christianity. Which helped me stay sober for a couple of years. But that fire, brimstone, and hard, righteous thinking did not agree with me. And I soon relapsed again. By the next time I cleaned up, I had two beautiful daughters (I did stay sober through both pregnancies)

It was 1995 (second rehab), and I knew that I needed a different path.

I remembered the lessons I learned from The Lord of the Rings and from Wicca; it fit for me because I was so close to the Earth; I loved it with my whole entire being, and I felt this was probably the right path for me.

I started to study with a shaman named Richard Gossett from Washington State. He was quite well-known, and I learned a lot from him. He and his assistants taught us the Celtic ways, which spoke to my inner Scottish heritage, and he crossed it with a mix of Wicca, which I felt was in alignment with who I was.

In April 1996, I was given my first Tarot deck, which also opened up a whole new world for me. I know the tarot back and forth, although I don't use it as much as I used to. It taught me about esoteric symbology and learnings. It is always a guide for me through numbers and has helped my path on the Medicine Wheel.

Wicca taught me how to live to love with the seasons, which is a very good way to live; it is also how our ancestors lived and brought one closer to the Earth.

By 1997, I was meditating every day and praying from the heart; throughout this journey, I will add that Jesus is still in my heart and always will be, just not in a traditional Christian religious sense. I have studied many books about his life and spoken to him through meditation on several occasions. It was at this time that I prayed to follow his way, The Way, which leans into the Essene or Gnostic teachings, which Jesus Ben Panther studied on his journey.

The day this prayer/mediation happened, I felt an unbelievable force of light enter me through the back of my neck and what I understand as the medulla oblongata area of the brain, which is connected to the spinal cord and the heart. It felt almost like a warm wind, and I saw the colors of blue and gold. This was the beginning of a very magical and almost overwhelming time of intuitiveness and healing abilities.

Creative juices were flowing through me like nothing I had ever experienced before. I started painting people I would see on my inner landscape, my guides. They turned out pretty good for a complete amateur, I was told. This year, I also created my first Spiritual Fair; I called it the Beltane Bash, for it was held on the original old Celtic holiday of May Day, usually held on May 1st.

All my fairs in the years to come were held at The Fort Langley Community Hall, and it was a great success. The whole concept was the inclusion of all faiths; the mission was to bring love, light, and harmony into my community and, hopefully, the world in general. My whole heart was in it to make a difference and to create healing and love.

There were all kinds of vendors selling their wares and different faiths spreading the word. From the Bahai's to the Rosicrucian's at one fair, we had nine different faiths under one roof and in harmony. Except for one of the local Christian churches, they decided to protest our fair and walked up and down the sidewalk telling people not to enter as they perceived our Fair as "Evil."

It was really bizarre, and for me, I felt deeply hurt. Those old Christian teachings were deep in me, and my love for the words of Jesus and what his mission was was very clear to me, and it did not include this hatred or negative energy. In 1999, I continued my mission and expanded my business; I was now doing the Goddess Fair for Autumn Equinox every year.

It was at this time that someone broke into my garage at home and wrote on the wall, "Exodus 22:18: 'Thou shalt not suffer a witch to live'". It was kind of scary for me as, by this time, I was a single Mom living on my own in Fort Langley. But I carried on, and in the year 2000, I opened my little metaphysical store called Mystical Moments across from the Community Hall. I started this basically on a wing, a prayer, and my Visa card!

I invited some of my vendors to participate, and we ran it as a cooperative selling our goods and services on consignment. One of these vendors was a real witch or a Bruja, and she sold spells and herbs. As we were all-inclusive, I didn't think much of it, although, in hindsight, I remember her husband painted our sign, which I had made in the shape of a hexagon, as the Star of David was a huge symbol for me. It represented the Christ way, and each point was a color of our chakra system for me and a direction on my personal medicine wheel. Above, Below, East, South, West, North, and the Center were spirit.

The logo I designed was seven hands in a circle in all the colors of the rainbow, which, to me, represented all faiths and races. But the husband had painted the hands with claw nails, which seemed kind of devilish. I painted over it because it felt wrong to me and painted my own sign, which was the sun, moon, and mountains.

We were only open for a few months when a friend of mine, who worked at the coffee shop next door, came over and asked me to speak about something serious. She told me that she had overheard a group of people who were from a local Langley Church talking about the store. They were actually in the process of filming a documentary on us! She actually saw them go across the street to the Community Hall and film the store. They were there for a few hours, she said.

I can remember that day. A number of young people came into the store and were going through the display of the woman who was a Bruja. They were actually quite rude to me when I asked them if I could help them. They stood there for at least a half hour going through the display and discussing what was on it. Unbeknownst to me, as I was busy with another customer, they were filming in the store!

As I mentioned before, some of my personal art was set in the frame of the Star of David, but somehow, in the documentary, they portrayed this star as an upside-down pentagram, saying it was a star of Satan.

I don't really know what ended up happening with that documentary, but I do know the head of that church (in Virginia)was arrested for being a pedophile a few months later. Then, not long after this, my store was egged, and again, the local paper came out to record it. By this time, I had been featured in two articles as an up-and-coming new business in

Langley. Most people understood my vision and loved the fairs and store atmosphere.

I was devastated by all this negative attention, and after seven years of sobriety, I started to imbibe some wine here and there. The store closed in 2001, and the last fair was in 2002.

This was the start of very dark times for me and the journey into the Dark Night of the Soul. By 2007, I had lost my home, my family, and everything you could imagine. I lived on the street for three years and even went to jail a few times.

On July 4th, 2010, I became clean in the same treatment center I went to in 1991. There is much more to this story, but I have kept it relatively short as this is just a chapter.

The persecution of me and my business brought up a lot of really negative feelings for me. I think probably even past life stuff when I lived as a witch in another lifetime. It took a few years to really manifest in my outer life but manifest it did.

I am now 14 years clean and sober. I went back to college when I was 50 and became an Addictions Counsellor, and I started all over again.

Today, I have a lovely home, two great daughters, two great sons-in-law, two wonderful granddaughters, and my cat Lucy. Currently, I work with Youth at Risk and have started my journey as a Wise Woman again.

I am setting up my mini Healing Center, doing healing circles and the good work required for our beautiful Earth and the realms of the Ancestors and Spirit world. I hope to bring love, light, and harmony into the world one day at a time and give many prayers for the world to live as one where all faiths honor and respect each other. I pray this in the name of the Mother, of the Father, and of the Great Spirit that binds us all.

"Scars mean you fought. Wrinkles mean you lived.
Heartache means you loved."
Matshona Dhliwayo

3

RECLAIM YOUR POWER: SO YOU CAN BE UNSTOPPABLE

WENDY BERGEN

"The strength of a woman is not measured by the impact that all her hardships in life have had on her; but the strength of a woman is measured by the extent of her refusal to allow those hardships to dictate her and who she becomes." C. JoyBell

My name is Wendy Bergen, and I have been asked to write about my life. What's neat about this is that I didn't know if I could do that a few weeks ago. Originally, when I agreed, I knew I could. I was feeling pretty great.

What you don't know is that I was diagnosed in May 2022 with stage 4 breast cancer that has metastasized to the bones. I've been doing great up until about four weeks ago. What happened was I hurt my back to such a point I was hardly doing anything; I could hardly move; the pain was so excruciating, and I couldn't even lift my arms to put a top on, and all I did was concentrate on releasing the pain.

They had to bring in-home support and told me the cancer had spread more into the bones. I was devastated. I have been Boldly causing miracles and magic, and I did not want to hear that the cancer had gotten worse. They are now talking about palliative care and hospice care.

My whole intention and purpose in writing this book is to make a difference and give women access to their own power. Fortunately for me, I've been having some movement for the last four days and can eat and move around, so here I go.

I feel so loved and appreciated by hundreds if not thousands of people. I am so grateful for my life, even with these diagnoses.

When I look at my past, it could have been so different if I had not started loving and trusting myself and others. You see, I had a violent upbringing. I was sexually violated, beaten, and betrayed by some of my caregivers. But now I have been able to forgive them.

I was born into a family of Alcoholics. My mom and dad were both Alcoholics and were very young. I think my dad was 17, and my mom was 19. They didn't have a lot of good coping skills, and there was lots of violence in our home.

At a young age, the four of us, my baby sister, my twin brother, and my older sister, were separated and put in different homes. Fortunately, my twin and I stayed together in foster care, where there was sexual abuse and unsafe conditions, which shaped my life.

Anybody who comes from trauma, whatever trauma it is, has a challenging life ahead until they recognize what they're dealing with. We need to be able to release the trauma so that we can have freedom and power.

When I was nine, my twin and I went to live with my dad. Dad was very unhealthy, and so was my stepmother. She had never had any children. My stepmom would beat me. my dad showed her how to strap me to not leave marks! They strapped me on my bum and my back with a belt buckle so people wouldn't see the marks.

When I was 15, my dad was sexually inappropriate with me, and finally, at the age of 15, I left to save my life. I was in the middle of grade ten, scared to tell anybody what I was dealing with because I didn't think I'd be believed. In the past, whenever I told people 'stuff,' my dad told them that I made it up.

He had enrolled all my relatives, and many people around me thought I was a liar. I was a storyteller, so no one would know what he was doing to me, so I grew up pretty angry and married young. I think I was 21, my first marriage.

Now, I coach women to be unstoppable and to Reclaim their power.

How do you become unstoppable when facing adversity? Now, I have a deep desire to pass on to the world a few things that might make a difference. I'm all about perception and turning our limiting barriers into clarity, freedom, and power.

My story begins with me being a very angry young woman. I had just left an abusive marriage and was working at the Sheriff's office. I didn't realize I was depressed and moody. A co-worker got angry with me and told me she couldn't stand me or my moods. She told me I complained about everything. She never knew if I was going to laugh, cry, or be rude, and she also threw in that nobody at work liked me; they just tolerated me. I was so hurt, and I truly believe she saved my life because she was so brutally honest.

When I reached out to a counselor at that moment, I learned I was pushing people away. I also learned I was an amazing, courageous woman.

At age 25, I took a transformational course that altered my life. "Landmark Worldwide". I am the author of my story. I did not have to live my life from my past beliefs; I excitedly learned that I could create and invent a future worth living in. How? The course concerns the blind spots that keep me from living a fulfilled life.

I continue to attend their seminars, which are the source of my living a powerful life regardless of any circumstances.

Part of my journey is to keep discovering any disempowering conversations I have about myself and the world in general. These conversations sabotage me and limit my ability to be free and powerful.

Some of them are,

- "I'm not lovable."
- "What's the use."
- "Why bother."
- "That's not fair."
- "I'm not smart."
- "I'm a failure."
- "I'm not good enough."

When you start recognizing disempowering conversations, you can choose differently.

After my first marriage, I got into another dysfunctional marriage, and it took a few dysfunctional relationships before I started doing the work that I really needed to do to love myself and discover what was driving me, and that continues to be an ongoing journey of discovering my blind spots.

If I'm not effective in an area, what am I blind to? That's where I find doing Landmark Worldwide Landmark Form and their seminars very powerful. I always keep myself in a seminar. I am working on my life not from there's anything wrong with my life. I live a very fulfilled life, but if I'm not as effective as I want to be in an area, there's something I'm blind to, and sometimes it takes a long time to see that stuff. You know, as you'll see, it's like we're these onion skins, and we have 300 million layers.

I've been doing transformation work for almost 45 years and keep on un-layering and un-layering. But what's really neat is that no matter what I've gone through, a second divorce, a third divorce, losing jobs, creating jobs, or ill health, I have had the opportunity to have freedom and power.

I'll share a little about how you create freedom and power.

These are some of the things I do so that no matter what my circumstances are, I have freedom and power. I could just share what I do. I'm always in a seminar with Landmarks Worldwide and take all sorts of other courses.

Energy work, all sorts of communication courses, and again, it's not that there's anything wrong with me, but if I want to be more effective and make a difference with others, then I need to be able to give them some access to their power.

One of the things that I ask my clients to look at is if they're facing any form of adversity. What are they committed to? Most of the time, when we look, we're more committed to being right about our view than what we are committed to.

If you want to know what you're committed to, look at your actions. If your actions aren't consistent with what you say you're committed to, you're blind to something. It's not bad, it's not wrong, but there's an impact.

Shall we start looking at the impact on me when I keep taking the same actions and keep being right about something? What's the impact on others? You see, something will shift if I keep looking at the impact. If I don't look at the impact, I'll keep taking the same actions and not being as effective as possible.

A simple example of an impact that I had not even seen was dealing with my older sister.

I have an older sister. We had a confrontation of some sort when my oldest child was like, I think, 12, and my sister, at that time. There weren't cell phones, etc., and she just said, "Don't bother to write, don't call, I don't want you part of my life."

I was devastated, and every year, I would call her, and she would say, "I don't know why you're calling; I don't need you in my life." This went on for approximately 27 years.

Then, the last time she said that, I said, "Well, I don't believe you have a fulfilled life because I'm not in it, and neither are your two nieces," and then I told her I loved her and hung up. A couple of weeks later, she texted me and asked if I would be interested in going down to Arizona with her. She had to drive her and her husband down there almost every year. Her husband was dealing with his mother's illness and couldn't go for a month, and she didn't want to drive by herself.

I said I needed to pray on it because I was still angry. We came to an agreement and started creating our relationship once again. It was a bit of a struggle at first, but I was down in Arizona for a month with her, and she flew me home and we've been building our relationship ever since.

Now, since I've been diagnosed with cancer that's metastasized to the bones and's gotten worse, my sister frequently will tell me how much she loves me. I noticed it because this is a blind spot when she tells me she loves me, and I have a hard time letting it sink in. Like it was, yeah yeah yeah yeah, and then and in the back of my mind, I would think, yeah, if you really love me, why haven't you apologized for not being in my life for 27 years and my daughter's lives?

I wanted to say, don't you get the impact that you were my everything, and all of a sudden, I wasn't allowed to be part of your life? What I realized was that in some of the work we do in landmark, it'll say if you have an upset, there's either an unfulfilled expectation, a thwarted intention, or an undelivered communication.

You can have all three or just one. What I saw was, you know, because earlier, I was talking about perception, and we frequently say we're committed. When I say I'm committed to family work, then I'm holding back letting my sister's love in, and I had never seen that, so my unfulfilled expectation was that she apologized to me.

Now, as long as I held on to that, she **should** apologize to me. No matter how frequently she said she loved me, I couldn't let her love in. It was just like Babble. I even thought that she would frequently do it when we were in groups together, and she would frequently do it in front of others. So in my head, I think you're looking good. You don't tell them how many years you weren't in my life, but now you're telling them what a wonderful sister you are.

I want you to know that she is a wonderful sister, and I love her greatly. Since I was diagnosed, my sister has been my biggest advocate. She is on every Doctor's appointment call. Even when she is on holiday, she sets aside the time. I sometimes have three or four appointments a week.

She is a retired social worker who worked in palliative care. She is also a therapist and still practices while she holidays and travels. She talks to my health team and ensures that my head palliative nurse is informed if something is missing. In fact, if it weren't for her fighting for me, I would not have the good care I do get.

When she is not on holiday, she lives about a four-hour ferry ride away and has shown up twice in emergencies to ensure I am not alone. Sometimes, people's words don't mean as much as their actions. This sister I can absolutely count on. She has willingly taken on being my executor and financial person, etc. It's a lot of paperwork.

She was that for our mother, who passed away two years ago. She fights to make sure everything runs smoothly. Her actions are way beyond what an apology would mean.

Holding on to my righteousness that she needed to apologize prevented me from letting her love in. I talked this over with a Landmark Form leader. I saw I was being inauthentic, saying I wanted families to work, and then I was holding back letting love in from my sister, who is going way beyond what she has to do to make my life work as I go through this journey.

I was holding onto an unfulfilled expectation. My sister didn't have the same perception as me. I asked myself if it really mattered. I realized it didn't matter. When I let that unful-filled expectation go. When I let myself release my right-eousness, I was finally free to let her love in.

Until then, I didn't see the impact on me or her. Not letting someone's love in is a pretty high impact. I'm so glad that I let that go, and now when my sister tells me, I totally get it. You know, I may be in my last few months of living my life, and what a breakthrough to realize that I was withholding love from the person I loved. That is what I call a blind spot, and one of the reasons why I do Landmark seminars and courses is that I'm always discovering new things I'm blind to.

I'm the author of my story, and if I want to live a fulfilled life, if I'm not letting love in, I need to discover why and choose freely instead of holding back or withholding my love or letting someone else love in.

So I'm going to ask you some questions, and if you answer them authentically, you might discover some blind spots yourself.

Where in your life do you have restrictions on your ability to express love? Where in your life are you holding back, justi-fying how you behave because someone hurt or offended you?

Where in your life are you right about someone, and that righteousness is stopping you from allowing someone's love in or stopping you from loving them? Can you recognize that your behavior and actions sometimes are very young? Do you ever regret behaving a certain way or acting in a certain way? Have you ever questioned why you said or did something? Perception shapes our actions.

If you alter your thoughts, you can alter your actions, and if you alter your actions, you can alter your world.

We are only as sick as our secrets.

I want to address addictions right now. You know my parents both were active Alcoholics, and when you live in that environment, you don't learn healthy relationship skills. Addiction is cunning, baffling, and powerful, and the people who are addicted don't believe that they have a problem.

I've heard many people say all my drinking doesn't affect anybody, but one of the things that people need to know is that we directly affect 25 people, so if we have an addiction problem, we are affecting 25 people. It isn't just us. The person or the people around the addicted person because the behavior is crazy-making. For example, you start something, and you start a conversation, and they want to argue. There's no reasoning that that sort of insanity and insanity permutates the whole relationship. Unfortunately, with addictions, you can't always trust what the person says because at the moment they say it, they mean it.

I want to share that we are only as sick as our secrets, and I will share a little bit. I was 36, actually, and I'd given birth to a beautiful baby girl, and her father was addicted to alcohol. The thing that you want to know about the insanity of addiction is whether the person who's addicted is addicted to the drug of their choice, alcohol or drugs.

Whatever, but the person who is just as crazy as the alcoholic can become as crazy because I was addicted to the addict. I was obsessed with trying to control the uncontrollable. So I became sick, and I did not know that I had an addiction, like the alcoholic who was my obsession with trying to control.

What was going on when we were together as a couple? I saw my stepchildren, 13 and 11, at the time we raised them, dry-humping each other. I got triggered because of a whole bunch of stuff from my past because I had been sexually abused. I brought it up to the attention of my daughter's dad, and he wouldn't believe me, and he wouldn't address it.

That frightened me, and I was told I should go to therapy, so I went to therapy. I think my daughter was eight months old when I started going to therapy. I had to drive from Hope to Vancouver every week. The therapist I went to was highly recommended. She worked with adult children of Alcoholics who have been traumatized and sexually abused. That was her specialty.

I couldn't remember being sexually abused; I had blocked that. I had triggers. I didn't have any memory of it when I went there. I said to her, "You know, I don't remember any sexual abuse." She said, "Well, let's work on what you are dealing with."

I was in a crazy relationship. She got me to come down on Sunday nights to join to

a group of women. It was called 'The Courage to Change'; about 25 of us were there. She said, "You know this is a two-year program, and we'll be lucky if there's a half-dozen of you at the end because it's a lot of work, working on yourself and looking at your part."

Every time I got an opportunity to share in this group I declined because I would hear all these women's stories. I could empathize with them but couldn't relate to certain things. In fact, I got triggered. I didn't know what to share when I noticed I got triggered. Then, one day, a young lady shared about her brother being harmed, and all of a sudden, I saw my twin.

We're in the foster home, and he was being harmed, and it started bringing stuff up for me, but I thought, well, I've been told so many times, if I said anything to my father, I was told I was lying, I was making stuff up so.

I said to the therapist, "How do I know that I just saw flashes? I didn't see whole pictures of stuff that flashes." I said, "How do I know I'm not making this up."

She asked, how old are you? I think I was three at the time that I saw the plan. She said, "Three-year-olds don't make that stuff up; you can trust yourself." That was the beginning of my healing. I had all this shame that I'd been married a few times. I had been in and out of relationships, and none of it worked. I had no self-worth. I kept secrets. I didn't share what authentically I was going through. I would be numbed out. I got addicted and obsessed with the man I was involved with rather than looking at my part in life.

I didn't know that, and so she recommended Al-Anon. At first, I was going to adult children of Alcoholics, and I found in that program for me, no one had to take any responsibility. It was always the parents' fault. But when I started going to Al-Anon, I started looking at my part and not keeping secrets. I got a sponsor and was terrified to share some stuff with her.

I worried she wouldn't want to be my friend if I shared some of the stuff. I shared this with her, and she laughed and told me something worse than she did, and I started to heal slowly. I started going to meetings regularly and started looking at why I was attracted to these Alcoholics in my life.

Every one of them was Charismatic and loving and smart and held jobs like a lot of people have. An idea that an alcoholic is a fall-down drunk, well they can be at times, but they are very functional. So it's a hidden disease; we don't see it, but it affects the whole family.

I did because I wasn't getting along with them. I would take it out on my child and bark at them. I wasn't present to them, I'd yell. If I was trying to please them and they weren't in a good mood, then when I wasn't in a good mood.

It's a really crazy-making, but what I want to emphasize is when I started sharing with safe people, I had so much shame that I've been married three times, I've been in and out of numerous relationships, and I had none of them work. It must be me, not that this has got to be me. I discovered that I had a part in it, and yes, I kept choosing those things because they were easier than dealing with my life! I thought if I looked at my life, I would break and start crying. I'd never stop crying, but we're stronger than we think.

We are, and even though I was going to Al-Anon and doing Landmark, I still got involved in relationships that weren't necessarily healthy. They were getting healthier, and each relationship got better and better, but I had to learn that I could live a life like this is the interesting part.

I was a successful entrepreneur. I owned my own store and didn't have to rely on a man financially. I had money in the bank and no debt, but I still kept choosing these people because I did not see myself as worthy. I saw myself as, you know, what I've been told most of my life from my family of origin. I was a useless, no-good liar and wouldn't amount to anything, etc.

I was, in fact, told many things that weren't true. And so I had, you know, looked in the mirror and didn't see this loving, incredible, awesome woman. I just saw this broken woman, and it was in the sharing; it took overtime, and this didn't happen overnight. It took over years.

I started seeing my patterns, and even now, that's why I do a lot of Landmark. I'm always looking at my blind spot to see what's missing. Not that there's anything wrong with me, but it's like, oh, something is missing here.

What am I stepping over? What am I not telling the truth

about? I learned to share with safe people. You know, I was so needy; I would pick people that were unhealthy and share with them, and then they would hurt me. Then, more evidence to not share. It's unsafe to share, and I had to learn to love myself. I learned that through several sponsors in Al-Anon, I like to share and get that I'm only as sick as my secrets.

If I can get this out to one person, I can share it with all they know. People have told me, "God, you reveal so much about your life and don't hold anything back." Why would I hold anything back that possibly could help someone else?

When we share responsibly, we do not know the impact on others. I know the other day, I was at Walmart talking to a lady, and I shared what I'm dealing with health-wise and told her how grateful I am for this. We got talking, and she said, "You made my day. Thank you for talking with me." I had no idea I just shared, but I intentionally share my life fully, and if it makes a difference for others, great.

I started to feel safe sharing the silly things I've done, my experience, strength, hope, and how God encouraged me. Once I stopped keeping secrets, my life started getting better.

I didn't tell people how bad it was at home. My youngest daughter's father would try to ensure I was isolated from others. He really made me feel and look wrong and rarely ever praised me. I stayed because I screwed up every relationship.

I had this shame that I had screwed up every relationship, and now I was going to screw up another relationship. So I stayed for 23-some-odd years. When should we have split after two weeks, or shouldn't we even have gotten together? If I was really honest, there were red flags right from the beginning, but I was looking for love in all the wrong places.

I could share with my sponsor, and I did a fourth step inventory every year. I tried to do that every year, looking at my part, not other people's parts. I started getting well, and when I started sharing and not worrying about what others thought, I started getting well. There's a saying in Al-Anon, 'We're only as sick as the secrets we keep.'

I believe that if we keep our secrets, we feel shame, and the spiral goes down. Whereas if we can openly say, hey, I was foolish; I was married four times or five times, or I did this, or I, you know, I drank alongside. I never did that because I can't consume too much, but don't be afraid to find safe people to share if you're sharing and people are judging you or they don't understand. Or if you're going to the wrong people.

It reminds me of when I always hurt and hurt people. I would seek out other hurt people because we connected, and then we'd end up hurting each other because the horns in their heads fit in the holes in mine.

I left that 23-year abusive relationship and did the work I needed to do on myself. I was 60 years old.

I'd been coaching people for over 30 years for free and discovered they were making money from my coaching, so I started charging. Since then, I have made amends on my part in the relationship, and my daughter's father is engaged and happy.

Our whole family, our children, spend important holidays together, and there is absolutely no friction. That took over five years before he started shifting his attitude toward me, but I kept responding rather than reacting. The most important thing for me was that no matter how old our children are, they need both parents. He is there for my daughters and granddaughter, and that's all I care about.

So, transformation happens when we start opening up and not keeping secrets. When we start sharing with others, we realize we are not alone. When we keep our secrets, we think we're alone. This is what I discovered in Al-Anon.

I've been asked to speak to others. When I share, people can relate to what I'm saying, and they don't feel alone. I think what keeps us in shame. Our secrets make us think we're bad, and then we don't share, realizing that other people go through the same stuff as we do. When we can share our growth and what we're learning we can help each other. So many people look into other people's lives and think they live such an awesome life, but they don't know what goes on behind closed doors.

So again, I can't emphasize we're only as sick as our secrets; when I started sharing, I started getting myself worthy. I started seeing what an amazing woman I was. I look back, and I think, 'Oh my God, I made those choices because I had a perception that whatever it was, it was a wonky perception, and the truth is I was this amazing, bright, brilliant young woman.'

I continue to be a brilliant older woman, and I share my wisdom so hopefully, this has given you some access to your power.

My intention in writing for this book was to make a difference. So that people have access to their own power.

Since I left my former 12 years ago, I have continued to be a successful entrepreneur. I am a transformation solution coach. I have successfully written a bestseller by myself called Getting Unstuck by Wendy Bergen. Brian Tracy and Kevin Harrington from Shark Tank endorsed my book.

When I wrote the book, I didn't publish it for a couple of years because I questioned if it was a valuable book, etc. Then, I had a good coach read it and say, I'm only on the first chapter. Even though Brian Tracy and Kevin Harrington had endorsed it, it's amazing to get this thing published. I still questioned myself until someone I trusted told me to be the publisher.

The fear is there, and I get to choose whether I take action based on the fear or take action from reality. I also have a 21-day challenge that makes an incredible difference and has people looking at themselves, being effective and fulfilling on a project that's important to them. I've been told it has saved lives.

Even though I'm going through this health journey, there are moments when I believe that God, if he so wishes, will release this cancer. If not, I will keep sharing my experience, strength, and hope and inspiring others so they can access their power and encourage them to get the help they need. Not because you're broken!

I invite you to look at yourself like a tree with all these leaves and branches, and as it grows and we trim it and take care of it, it shines and thrives. If we don't water it and take care of it, we shrink. So I want you to get that you can thrive and grow. You are not broken. It doesn't matter what you have gone through you can have freedom and power. Look at me if I can do it, you can do it.

I am one of seven people in the world certified to lead a course called 'Reclaim Your Power' RYP, which is all about the disempowering conversations that leave us ineffective. It isn't about not having negative conversations or disappearing conversations. It's about how quickly you can catch those conversations, stop reacting to them, and start responding and choosing another conversation that would empower you. But first, you have to get those words to create our world. So, we need to be more aware of what we're speaking and what we're saying to ourselves.

I strongly believe that if you alter your perceptions, you alter your actions, and you can alter your world. Most of you don't believe you have beliefs that limit you. You think they are the truth, and you're willing to go to war to prove you're right.

Just look at your world. Look at your relationships with your family, your neighbors, your coworkers, and your husband. What could become available in the world if you and others globally recognized that you are stuck and that we can get each other unstuck globally? So, my words are to cause you to pause, ponder, and question your thoughts. If you alter your thoughts by interrupting and questioning them, you can alter your actions. Most of us do not question our thoughts; therefore, we stay stuck.

I believe it takes a lifetime to master transforming our thoughts. Picture every moment you have as an opportunity to question yourself: does this thought limit me? Is this creating a limiting barrier?

Consider the experiment of fleas in a jar. The fleas jump high to get out, but they can jump no further because the jar has a lid. Eventually, the fleas never tried jumping higher because they are trained; they have a limiting belief that has become an invisible barrier.

You are just like that flea; you also have that invisible barrier. You frequently stay in your comfort zone, therefore creating your own stuckness and limiting your circumstances.

It is my honor to meet you through this book. I hope we can meet in person one day. Thank you for reading. When you're finished, please pass along a copy to your friends, family, and co-workers so you can make a positive difference in their lives.

Where are you keeping secrets?

If you are not thriving in an area, do you know where to go for resources? What do you react to? Do you react to what people say or how they say it?

In other words, what lessons have you learned from break-downs when you look at an area where you're not being as effective?

"Great things never came from comfort zones."
Neil Strauss

4

THE STRONG ONE: ONE DIES, ONE SURVIVES AND THE STORY IN BETWEEN

DARLENE LONGO

"Above all, be the heroine of your life, not the victim."
Nora Ephron

People tell me they see a strong woman when they look at me, and I guess I am, but I don't really see myself that way. I guess it's about perspective, and I've become strong, but it didn't start out that way. Yeah, I've been through a lot, but then who hasn't? A rite of passage struggle is, isn't it?

Recently, I was asked to write a story about who I am and how I got here. There is so much to tell, so many stories, and tough, heartbreaking stuff, so where to start? The beginning seems as good a place as any.

I was born in a suburb of Toronto, Canada, a big city. I believe my grandparents were Italian, and my parents were born in Canada. They met at a dance club in Toronto, and as the story goes, my father was completely smitten with my mother.

She was stunning. Of course, he was. She wasn't keen on him, though he was quite handsome, but her family urged her to marry him, as he had a very good work ethic and some ambition.

He took an electronics course at an early age and became an appliance repair man for most of his life, a respectable job. My mother and he began to have children immediately. She would have six, although only five would survive.

We were pretty Canadianized by the time our generation was born. Even losing the Italian language, sadly.

In my immediate family, I had an older sister, two older brothers, a younger brother, and me in the middle. Me, I was borne of tragedy, and I wasn't born alone. I had a twin sister. And though she didn't live much more than three months, her death was shrouded in mystery.

Her official cause of death was SIDS, the sleeping death.

My mother, however, had been ill and not the kind of illness that was talked about. In hushed whispers and being whisked off to foster care. We spent a lot of our time shuffling in and out of foster care as a direct result of my mother's illness, which would fluctuate in her lifetime.

When she came home from the hospital, she would always be given meds that she would take for a short time and then slowly slide back into her illness.

Some of those times in foster care were really horrible for me, being separated from my siblings as well as being bullied by some of the other kids because I was very sensitive and cried a lot.

Even as I went back home to be with my siblings, I remember following my sister around like a puppy, crying all the time for her attention. However, she was seven years older and was quite annoyed by that. My elder sister and I shared a room.

I remember trying to chat with her at night, and she would tell me to shut up. I would say, "It's okay, just knowing you're there; it's fine." And I would chatter away to her while she turned her back on me and went to sleep.

She was always quite intolerant of me, although she did have her moments of kindness towards me. For example, she made me a peasant dress when I was about 12 years old, which I still remember fondly. The fabric was a peasant dress I picked out with big plaid hearts on it.

I loved that dress, and even as I outgrew it, I cut out the hearts to use as patches on my jeans until I outgrew the jeans, too. Perhaps those plaid hearts symbolized love to me—the one thing I craved but could never quite find.

Anyway, the gesture of her doing that dress for me meant a lot to me. We have a very strained relationship, and despite that, it still holds a special place in my heart.

Eventually, my sister, overwhelmed with the family, left home before I hit puberty. I remained to fend for myself in a houseful of boys. My mother, by then, was in and out of lucidity, her illness aggressively overtaking her.

I recall in horror getting my period and being afraid to tell anyone. Stuffing Kleenex and toilet paper into my panties for months until I finally told my father I needed a few dollars to get supplies. Then, having to explain to him what kind of supplies I needed. As a young girl, I was mortified, yet we did this every month until I finally started making my own money. Babysitting for the neighborhood kids and then a job as the fitting room girl in a local dress shop.

I spent a lot of my time alone. I just accepted my other half had a different destiny than I did. I thought of my twin often and wondered why I had survived and she had not. What did it mean?

Back then, I had terrible nightmares of suffocating, and for years, I remember waking up gasping for air, terribly afraid. We had been identical twins. I never told anyone. This reoccurring night terror followed me for most of my childhood.

My childhood progressed in and out of foster care, and then back home with my unwell mother and hard-working father. My father struggled to raise his five children, keep food on the table, and manage my mother. That resulted in many fights and things, being broken and screaming at night, and all of us kids scattering in different directions and hiding.

I remember my father telling my mother that he was going to leave and me running to him, sobbing and pleading, "Daddy, don't leave me! Don't leave me!" Then he'd pick me up in his arms as I was crying, hold me, and say, "Honey, I'm never gonna leave you." Years later, on his deathbed, I reminded him he'd promised. As I cried inwardly, I knew that this time, he had no choice.

My father always stayed for us, fought for us, and always won us back from foster care. If I ever felt love, it was from my father.

My siblings were paired off: my older sister and brother and my other two brothers, who shared a room. I was often on my own, pondering the idea that I was missing my other half.

My mother, during this time, often acted out when I was around. She told me fantastical stories of how my twin sister was kidnapped and a TV star. She sometimes would even point out a child on TV and say, "Look, there she is." Though this confused me, I never believed her. I knew they were lies. Though I really wanted to believe that she was out there and that someday I would find her, I knew better.

Then, in a brief moment of happiness on my birthday, my siblings would remind me. "I wonder what it would be like if Charlene (my deceased other half) was here?" Any happy moment I had at that precise second evaporated, and I was filled with overwhelming loss.

My birthdays to this day are haunted by that loss. Like a record player, I cannot turn it off. What if... I believe that I mourned every single moment the loss of my twin, my play-mate, my confidant lost forever.

My mother acted out in other ways when I was around, sometimes sinister and frightening. I once found her crying in her breakfast cereal, and I looked at her and told her she was loved, and she looked at me with daggers and came at me, picked up a chair, and hurled at me as I clambered to get out of my own chair and fell. That chair hit me as I was fleeing on the back of the leg. I ran out of the house, not looking back with no understanding that I had somehow triggered something deep inside of her.

I wondered if there was something else going on. I spent a lot of my childhood terrified of my mother.

Then, when I grew older, one day when I felt really safe and no longer lived at home. I suddenly realized she had murdered that baby, my twin!

The memory shot into my mind like a movie picture. I stopped in my tracks. I was with some friends, and just moments before, we had been laughing and joking, and they looked at me quizzically. I said under my breath. "Oh, she killed the baby, "but I did not say it aloud. I couldn't tell them!

I would have to explain everything about my mom I'd sought so hard to keep secret thus far. I couldn't do that!

However, for the first time in a long time, I felt strangely calm and not the least bit afraid. Remembering had freed me somehow. The realization came quietly and without fear, something I believe I had known all along deep inside me.

My mother was not a cruel, mean person, but just unable to cope, and the crying babies became too much for her.

The story I heard was that she couldn't cope when the twins came along, she couldn't cope. She would leave us unfed and soiled in our bassinets until my father would arrive home from work at the end of his workday. Only then would we be fed and changed. It was quite apparent my mother was not coping at all by this point.

As sure as I stand before you, I knew all of this at that moment, and I was okay. I understood. When I realized consciously that she had suffocated that child. I also knew. She had known I knew it. I had been the silent witness in the bassinet right beside my suffocated twin.

I recall a story I had been told when my mother had left my father briefly. She had packed a bag and was walking down the street, so my father put all of the children in the car to go find her, pleading with her to come home. She had called her sister and said, "I'm afraid to go back. I'm afraid something bad will happen." Something bad had happened!

How awful must it have been for her in her lucid moments to realize what she had done? Then to have me always there reminding her. Somewhere along the way, I forgave her, but I was very angry for a long time before the truth truly sank in.

When my memory was buried deep inside, I was angry with her for being weak, unwell, and unable to care for us. I feel differently now. These days, I think of my lost twin as a guardian angel.

She has gotten me out of many jams along the way. I am thankful for that. Now, when I go a little astray, I ask that she tell God to show me mercy. As I have done with the memory of my mother. As guardian angels go, it appears mine is steadfast and true.

As for my mother, she was not an evil person; she was ill. I do have some fond memories of my mother, though few. Perhaps not loving, but caring. She did needlepoint, she painted. She made lemon tarts and mincemeat tarts every Christmas, small things, I know. Perhaps that was all she could give us, but she did try.

I can't imagine being totally overwhelmed with five children and a mind that was slipping more and more each day. Her everyday life is just too much for her to deal with.

I don't know what caused her illness. I know very little about her past before my father. Although I did meet her sisters and brother as a child, I heard few stories I can recall. Some stories state she was incredibly beautiful and taken advantage of before my father came along.

I don't know for sure, but I wonder what it must've been like to live inside her head. Perhaps daily fighting with yourself just to survive that reality until it becomes so incredibly painful, you just slip into an entirely different world.

That, from the eyes of a child (this child), looks terrifying.

We talk about mental illness so loosely, so removed, clinically. I have been told lots of things about mental illness in my lifetime. From "it's hereditary, maybe you'll get it too." Like it's cold, I might catch, too," People who are ill are okay, just different, nothing to be afraid of."

In my experience, they can be unpredictable and even dangerous. The problem is you don't know when that will be. This does not define all mental illness, just my experience. It does make you wary naturally.

Most, I think, are not any different than you and I. We might have a better grasp on reality, but as I said once to someone who I know had once slipped, "Does that make them ill or us?"

Perspective is like weakness or strength. It's all about where you are standing and who is looking on. So far, my sanity is intact. Does that make me strong? Am I strong?

My brother reminds me that it was I who was in the incubator for two weeks before I came home.

I had been the weak one, least likely to be here now. Yet I had survived, overcome the odds. He said that I would always be a survivor. And I admit, though there were many times I wanted to throw in the towel, I remember all the work it has taken just to get this far, so it's doubtful I would ever give up now.

"You need to make good on what God gave you, for you were not born without purpose." Yes, my words. Now, to define what that purpose is. Only you can do that!

Perhaps it is the birth of a child that you never thought you would have because it wasn't something you ever wished for, but the universe gave it to you—a gift. Maybe that is your purpose. Maybe it's to write your story like this. Your story so that it can reach other people who are struggling.

Feeling less than. When they are so very much more than they are believing or feeling at that moment, oh, but feelings are fickle, thank goodness. Go forward like a warrior! Even when you aren't feeling it. That is strength. Your words may help someone to heal and understand.

Imagine this: if our trauma helps us understand and lift each other up, perhaps in the end, it was a gift, even if it was a strange and painful one.

You can survive all of it and thrive still! Like me. Yes, I am strong—much more than I ever thought I would be. Through many tribulations in my life, it's held true. Even when I was broken, I was strong. I didn't see it; lucky for me, others did.

So, I remember these words on days I'm not feeling it.

"I am strong, I am invincible, I am woman!" Helen Reddy

These words were never truer than now. These words were never uttered or sung so brazenly loudly as when sung collectively. We are strong women, all of us!

"Although the world is full of suffering, it is full also
of the overcoming of it."
Helen Keller

5

OUR LOVE STORY: IN MEMORY OF CHRIS MASON

TRACEY GRAVES

"You know you're in love when you can't fall asleep because
reality is finally better than your dreams."
Dr. Seuss

Friday, May 17th, 2002 (known as the May "24" weekend) is
the day I saw a man on a dancing machine at a hockey arena
in Pierrefonds, QC. He had already captured my heart by
Sunday, May 19th, 2002.

I had vowed to myself that after a very abusive relationship
with my son's father, I was not going to become involved with
anyone ever again. My defense wall was very high, and I was
determined never to let anyone in again; it was too dangerous.
Friday May 17, 2002, was Victoria Day Weekend and the
start of our hockey tournament. I was Assistant Coordinator
for a AAA Hockey Tournament for Division 1 and Division
2 schools in the USA, working with Scouts to seek out excep-

tional talent for their elite schools. We had teams in from all over Ontario, Nova Scotia, and Quebec. It was busy, and I didn't have a lot of time on my hands...until he spoke to me.

Ever get the feeling someone is watching you? I could sense it constantly but didn't pay any attention to it, after all this was about hockey. I watched as he danced with his daughter and teammates from the Kingston Beasts Hockey Team, thought to myself how lucky these girls were to have such a fun dad hang out with them.

At the end of the first night, as everyone returned to the hotel, I found myself in the bar, just wanting a cigarette (I had been trying to quit, and yes, you were allowed to smoke in the bars then) and a cold beer. I stood at the bar, sipping away and chatting with some of the parents, and another drink appeared. I thanked the bartender, and he said, "Thank the gentleman over at that table," he was there alone. With a big smile on his face and a Cigarillo in his hand, he raised his glass (signature Rusty Nail), and I walked over to thank him. The love story begins.

Our Love Story

After the Hockey Tournament ended, I was left with a business card (I still have it 22 years later). Life resumed, hockey mom and taxi service, back to work, and "loving life," so to speak. One day, I found that business card and wondered...do I call or don't I? I took a chance one day in late June 2002, and he answered the phone!

I was a babbling fool and pulled myself together quickly to remind him of who I was. I honestly wanted to know more about how to get out of the debt I was in ($3,000 – something I wasn't proud of), he offered, and I sent him everything he requested regarding my financial situation.

I obviously wasn't a top priority, and it took a couple of weeks to hear back from him. What he came up with was, in my mind, CRAZY. I had to live out of envelopes and no more credit cards unless it was an absolute emergency. Envelopes of life, all expenses, and a mere budget for entertainment. How would I balance that, plus my son and his best friend who lived with us? My son's best friend needed a safe place to live. I provided it to him, and his father was allotting monthly money to cover expenses.

Was it easy? Not at all, but that also meant we started speaking to one another more often. That's when the original messenger was popular, so we would chat on the phone when time allowed while he was at work or send messages to each other while I was at work (I will be very honest in saying I ran to the library five days a week on my lunch to be able to chat with him via messenger). We truly became good friends, talking a lot about my life and his life, and it pained me to realize how deeply unhappy he had been with his situation and how it happened.

As the spring turned to late summer, he was officially preparing to be on his own; a lot of dynamics went with this, including his kids leaving. It was a mess, and we chatted more frequently as he started to lose friends (a common theme with so many things). We started chatting in the evenings; he needed a friend. I was there and more than willing; I am a "helper."

He asked if I would be willing to drive to Cornwall to hang out, and he really needed to talk to someone. I lived much closer to the destination than he did, but we spent a couple of hours together, and I brought home a container of stew that Chris had made (I still have the Tupperware container; it brings back lots of memories). To say that it was the worst stew I had ever had in my life is an understatement, but he was so proud; I lied and said it was fantastic; many years later, I told him the truth – we laughed pretty hard, did I mention; he became a fabulous cook with lots of practice?!

Chris was so easy to speak to. He listened and heard everything I said...I didn't admit to him that when I walked into a room and he was there, my heart pounded wildly, but it wasn't the time nor the place, and perhaps it never will be.

My best friend Lina was starting to ask a lot of questions because I was "out of town" a lot. I took her into confidence and told her all about this man I met and was quickly falling for. She made me promise to let her know when she could meet him; after all, was he up to her standards (spoken like a true friend)? He knew all about Lina, and I let him know that I had spoken to her about him as well.

As time continued, Lina and Chris finally met, and she was in love with him immediately and he of her. We didn't allow anyone else to meet him then; our relationship was already changing, and no one needed to know.

My birthday was one week away from Christmas, and he felt bad that he couldn't be in Montreal. He arranged to have a card and money sent to Lina for me (yes, I still have the card) and instructions to take me out for dinner on him. We went to our local pub called PJ's and ordered drinks and munchies; then she presented me with a gift. He knew I wanted to buy a new pair of jeans, but because I was so determined to get out of debt, I didn't allow myself the pleasure.

In the card, he wrote that he was sorry he couldn't be there in person but wanted me to buy those jeans and enjoy my evening. I remember my heart soaring and tears trickling down my cheeks. I knew I was madly in love with this man, my Knight in Shining Armor.

2003, what a whirlwind. Everyone knew something was happening because I was not around very much. We couldn't stop it from happening. Dating was inevitable even though it was long distance. Living on the 401 Highway was neither easy nor fun, but the result was being together. We slowly introduced Chris to my family and friends; he was the talk of the town, so to speak, and everyone loved him. I knew I was deeply in love with him, but I didn't say anything to him. He was working through a separation, a house to sell, and finding a place to live. He didn't want to lose his business or his children, so I kept my feelings to myself and continued to be that close friend he needed.

May 2003: The separation agreement was signed. Chris moved to the apartment on July 1, 2003, and the house sold in August 2003. Our relationship continued to flourish. When he moved into the apartment, he was so proud and had very little. I visited on July 1, 2003, just for a day, but I truly never wanted to leave. Just being together, lying on a sleeping bag outside to catch some sun, was enough for me to know where I wanted to be.

2004, I decided it might be the time for a career change, but I had no idea what interested me. Chris arranged for me to meet with a Career Councillor in Kingston to complete a career assessment, tailor my resume, and learn more about how to network in Kingston for a possible transition (yes, we were already discussing the possibilities of moving in together one day).

One of my passions was fundraising and event management; sure enough, the career assessment pointed me in that direction. I enrolled in online distance studies at Algonquin College for Conventions and Meeting Management, with a minor in Fundraising. I knew it would be a lot with full-time work, full-time mom, and school, but I began the journey with two courses. I quickly realized it was too much, but I completed them and enrolled for one each semester moving forward. I am not a math guru by any means, but Chris was, and he thrived on it; he was willing to help me with the budgeting portions of my assignments, and this was when more fun began.

My heart grew bigger each time we were together, but I knew

I couldn't say anything until one day over a turkey club, beer, and an assignment we were working on together (Chris used to laugh at my rolling eyes when it came to numbers). He said he needed to speak to me, and my heart sank; he saw the look on my face and held my hand. Here it was one of the best things to ever happen was about to end, or so I thought. He looked at me intently and said he had wanted to say something long ago but had to wait for the dust to settle with the divorce. The anticipation was killing me as I braced for the worst; he stumbled for words and finally took a deep breath to tell me that he fell in love with me the first day he met me in Montreal in 2002.

He had no idea what to do with it at the time because of his situation; he thanked me for being there for him through a rough time and said he loved me. I had tears in my eyes, and I had no idea what to do or say at that moment, except I wanted to stand on the table and shout out to the world that I was deeply in love with him. Instead, he wiped away my tears, and I looked at him and said, the first time I saw him on the dancing machine, I felt a ping but pushed it away. But the moment I thanked him for the drink, I was already feeling something stir and knew I was in love with him even though it was taboo. We had no idea what to do with these feelings, or us for that matter, but there it was in the open. We admitted how much we loved each other and that it was love at first sight.

The official divorce was in August 2004. Even though the world knew about us at this point, we took the time to just be together. We golfed in tournaments in Montreal but always made sure there was at least one escape weekend a month that was just us; how I miss those adventures. We trudged through snow, sleet, and hail to be together; weather wasn't stopping us. That summer, his oldest daughter moved in with him; she had been living in many different places; she was in school and felt she needed permanent accommodation. Chris brought her to Montreal for Christmas that year, and my family made sure that she was very welcome...oh the memories.

On April 15, 2005, Chris was in Montreal for a conference and requested that we stay at the hotel where we met, Holiday Inn Pointe Claire. I was down and out with a bad cold but agreed to go, and I slept while he was busy. We went to our favorite Brasserie for dinner and hid from the world, our cherished thing to do. That night, during one of our long conversations over a couple of drinks in our room, Chris got down on one knee and asked me to be his wife.

I cried, I screamed, and, of course, said yes; he had no ring but, in true Chris fashion, had a twist tie ring ready for me. The next day, we went to Jean Guy Aubrey in Dorval; a local jeweller our family had known for many years. There, we chose a beautiful one-of-a-kind ring that was made in-house. He placed it on my finger, and again, the tears rolled down my eyes.

We walked along the Lachine Canal hand in hand, both of us on top of the world. He wanted to visit my dad; the two of them had a deep admiration for each other, and he wanted to do the proper thing and ask my dad if he could make an honest woman out of me (yes, he actually said that, lol). Of course, this led to the dowry question, lots of laughter, and my dad crying because he never thought I would ever be so happy. Sadly, my mom had Alzheimer's, but when I showed her the ring, she started to cry. That night, we had Lina and her husband Serge over and told them; I've never seen anyone so happy for me; she was already making plans.

We rented a cottage with friends and my parents in Ste. Jovite Quebec, we explored Mont Tremblant, went to the beach, and had a great time. This was an opportunity for everyone to truly get to know Chris, the love of my life. Chris and I were still living on the 401, and Morrisburg became our home away from home. We had already started to discuss moving in together and our dreams, so many dreams. Owning a home, not a house, being there for our kids and grandchildren, and walking through our careers and expectations, I couldn't have asked for a perfect match.

In January 2006, my landlord sent a notice that he was not renewing my lease due to family members moving into the dwelling. This was stressful as I had to figure out where I was going to live and what about my son. His friend was moving out in March, so I didn't have to worry about his well-being at that point.

My son and his girlfriend announced they were moving in together; another problem was solved. Chris and I spoke at great length. Maybe this was the time. I discussed it with my parents; sadly, my mom already had Alzheimer's, so it was a tough subject to approach; she cried like a baby, which, of course, made me cry, and my dad, how would he do this on his own (yes, I felt guilty). With their blessing, I could move in with them and my cats for a period of time until my shifts were all covered at the hospital.

July 1, 2006, two trucks were in front of my home: one for my son and the other one for me. I was a mess leaving him behind, but he gave me his word that he would be alright and would look after his grandparents. Six of us left with the truck, a car, and a van filled to the brim to its new home in Kingston: 106-828 Sutton Mills Court.

September 1st, 2006 was the final move. Lina and I were in my car with the two cats with us. Serge had the balance of my items in his van, and Chris rode with him (he had taken the train to Montreal). The truck with my life in it was driven by Tommy and Katrina. Saying goodbye to my parents and son was hard, but I was about to start my new life with the man of my dreams, the one I had waited for my entire life. Lina, Serge, Katrina, and Tommy stayed the weekend to help us put the rest of the items together. It was a great time, but I didn't want to let them go. My entire life was in Montreal, and here I was, new to a small town I now called home. I had taken a one-year leave of absence from my position at the hospital; I moved to Kingston with no job but a few prospects.

In February 2007, after six months of applying for jobs and going to multiple interviews, I finally received an offer from the Heart and Stroke Foundation and Easter Seals for part-time contracts. It wasn't ideal, but it was a start. I loved my job at the Heart & Stroke Foundation, working with schools and kids promoting healthy activities, Jump Rope and Hoops for Heart. Easter Seals I had events that I was responsible for, but I didn't enjoy the office dynamics half as much. With regret, I had to leave the Heart and Stroke Foundation in July because they couldn't offer me full-time hours. I was devastated because I loved it that much, but I had to do what was best for Chris and I.

As time continued, we saw our kids grow up and move on to bigger and better opportunities: Nadine to England to teach, Corinne to Winnipeg to become a Professor, Adrienne to Australia to become a Nanny, and Terence to work in Kingston as an equipment operator. It looked like things were falling into place. The one thing Chris and I always agreed on was taking care of our kids and our parents first, then us. That might have been the beginning of some of our dreams falling apart.

In October 2007, I started a new job at Manpower, which was fantastic for the first eight years; my boss was amazing; we all became friends. Sadly, when she was walked out the door in 2015, life became very difficult; I only tolerated my new boss and the employee she hired. They both made me feel inferior, and the next two years were filled with anger, tears, and resentment.

My mental health was in very bad shape by the time I was finally let go in September 2017; it was a dream come true for me because I couldn't take it anymore. When I was handed my envelope, I cleaned out the rest of my desk (I had already started to because I had decided to give in my two weeks' notice when I was taking my Christmas holidays); I honestly didn't feel like I owed anything more than that, but this made it easier.

I went to see Chris at his office, and he did a double take. The look was priceless. He realized what had happened, and he closed his door. The smile on his face was wonderful. I could feel tension roll off his shoulders; it was really nice to see. We made an appointment with a labor lawyer but were certain that the package provided was perfect, but a second opinion was warranted.

In 2010, we secured what we considered to be our home away from home. A beautiful cottage in Lyndhurst, Ontario, on Bass Lake. We took it site unseen and never regretted it. Chris was terrified that I would go a bit on the loopy side because I get bored very easily. We brought our golf clubs, workout equipment, books, puzzles, and games.

Quite the contrary, we opened the door and dropped our bags; it was better than the pictures with large windows, an open-concept kitchen, a living room, and a dining room (which faced the lake). The porch was huge, and it was where we watched the sunrise every morning and the sunset at night. We learned how to use the camera that Chris had bought me (which I have forgotten how to use). We started each day watching the sunrise and drinking coffee (perhaps I had some baileys with mine, lol). Then we would crawl back into bed, being beside each other and holding on tight, which was something we enjoyed immensely. Did we feel like we were wasting the day? Absolutely not, we would sit outside, read, go for long walks, and cook meals together.

Our custom for almost ten years was to do a puzzle with at least 1,000 pieces (we were addicted to them, unable to stop once we started). We sat outside and read, lay in the sun, and forgot the world existed; we would play music and dance under the stars.

We started going for two weeks at a time. It just never seemed to be enough. Pre-Covid, we discussed taking weeks that people weren't able to go to anymore, to the point where we thought we could travel into Kingston for work and go back to the cottage every day. What a dream that was.

In 2020, things changed forever. The couple decided to pack it in and retire. Not only did we feel so isolated, but the one thing that kept us going was knowing we could escape the world. We frantically looked for somewhere else, but with the rules, it was difficult and very expensive. 2019 was the last year we went to the cottage, forever etched in my mind as we held hands in the dark with flashlights and hi-vis vests, walking country roads.

Chris became a very heavy drinker, and on our first Easter weekend, when we decided not to travel to see our parents in 2012, he disappeared. He went to a friend's place and drank until he passed out. I was furious and had packed a bag. I wasn't going to continue to tolerate his yelling and belligerence. He was not the man I had fallen in love with, and it reminded me way too much of my past, minus the violence, but there were a lot of heated conversations.

He came home mid-morning and was staggering drunk; I couldn't believe he had driven home in that condition; he didn't understand why I was so angry, and when he saw the suitcase, he knew I was no longer kidding. I told him I was leaving; I had found a hotel where I could take the cats and was out of there. He begged me to sit and talk to him; I gave him an ultimatum; I honestly didn't even listen to what he had to say at this point; I told him he either sought help or we were through.

He stormed out of the living room and slammed the bathroom door. I could hear the shower, and I waited to see what would happen next; he came into the living room with tears in his eyes. He allowed me to call EAP, and an emergency meeting with a counselor was set up who then directed him to AA.

He kept that very quiet, even from me; with time, he started to change; he was hanging out with another woman who I didn't trust even though he assured me there was nothing going on; he just needed the support. I honestly wanted things to work out between us but was having some trust issues now; our dream life was gone.

Admittedly, I, too, started to drink very heavily when he was because I felt like I had to keep up with his lifestyle; the difference was I didn't drink during the day; but he had started to, and it was affecting his ability to do very many things. Grateful for him starting with his meetings and therapy, it seemed to have calmed our life down and etch towards a new lifestyle.

Easter 2017 was such an exciting time for us. The kids were coming to Toronto with our grandchildren! We didn't tell his mom because we wanted it to be a surprise. Ever since Dad Mason passed away in 2014, she hadn't been the same person. We took her to East Side Mario's, her favorite place to have Hawaiian pizza. As they all strolled in, the tears of joy were unbelievable. We hadn't seen her smile like this in a very long time; it was perfect.

Chris and I had rented a hotel room, and the kids had an Airbnb; we visited Ripley's Aquarium the following day, took them shopping, and headed back to Kingston. They would follow in a couple of days, and we had a lot to prepare for. We purchased Easter baskets, toys, goodies, and eggs to hunt for. We invited our friends Adam and Candy to come over with their daughter Avelynn for the egg hunt and what a great time we had.

We went to the Annual Turkey Fair in Lyndhurst after I had been let go at the end of September 2017. We did our usual visit with friends, shopped at the local vendors, and went out for a canoe ride together; I have an extreme fear of boats but have been trying to conquer that for many years.

Chris was willing to hold my hand like he always did. We bumped into a friend of his, and we chatted for a bit; she asked how my job was going, and I let her know I was no longer employed. She quickly looked at her email and asked me to send her my resume. We exchanged information and continued our day. I was excited but didn't let my hopes get too high.

I was hoping that maybe I would get an opportunity for a part-time position. Not one week later after sending her my resume, I received a call from the HR manager to set up an interview.

In early October, I had my interview and filled out the necessary documents to do my Government Clearance. Time continued to tick, and I thought nothing was going to come of it. We had a trip planned to Arizona for Chris to attend a conference, so I would continue my job search when we returned home. There was a bit of correspondence as I had sent an email to the manager to advise her of my trip in the event they needed to speak with me. In the last week of October, we left for Arizona. We weren't even there 24 hours, and I received the email: I was hired, and my start date would be December 4, 2017. Our excitement was through the roof. Finally, the job that would help provide more stability to our lives, that home we dreamed of, and those trips we desired were now more attainable.

From February 29th to March 8th, 2020, Chris and I were lucky enough to score tickets to Tim Horton's Briar in Kingston. I am not a curler, but this was an experience not to be missed; Chris loved curling and, with pride, told me what was happening when he didn't think I had a clue (he knew me all too well). We spent time in the arena and the Briar Patch. Team Canada won, and the city went wild.

March 16th, 2020, one week after the Briar, the world shut down; we were not allowed to go out or socialize, stores and businesses were closed. We were basically prisoners with no rights, as time went on and things continued to change.

I continued to work from home, and Chris had to go into the office, deemed essential. Everything is a blur, to be honest; we lived in an apartment; my office was on the dining room table where we ate, and I couldn't sleep at night and wasn't allowed to go anywhere because of the fear of contracting COVID-19. I am a severe asthmatic.

This left Chris to do everything outside of the home, so I made sure to take care of everything inside the home, but it was taxing for him; if he contacted Covid, he couldn't see his mom. As time continued and we were allowed to be in a bubble, noticeable changes were happening to everyone. A fear like no other, panic, begging for vaccines, and a life outside of this madness. Countless times, Chris had to make the trip to Markham on his own because they were only allowing one person into the long-term residence.

In May 2020, we started to seriously look at homes; we had been the entire time we were together, but knowing I would likely be working from home for an undisclosed period, the arrangement was taxing on me; I became miserable. We weren't sure if it was the right thing or the wrong thing to do, but we needed more space.

As time allowed, we visited a few homes during a market that was becoming volatile. We walked into our current home and immediately fell in love; we weren't allowed to touch anything, only the real estate agent, but the more we saw, the more we knew that this was home. We were outbid, but at the encouragement of our real estate agent, we wrote a note to the sellers that won their hearts.

We had gone out for a walk, waiting for news, and the phone rang: in the middle of Appledown Avenue in Kingston, we screamed, we jumped, we shouted. Another new beginning for us. The moving date was Wednesday, September 16th, and we were prepared; another exciting chapter was about to begin. The deck was perfect, the sun faced the right way (we were sun worshipers); and no more darkness after work.

Our first Christmas in the house, we decorated our tree together, watched Christmas Vacation while wrapping gifts and enjoyed each other's time together; Chris had started to work more often from home. It was heaven; funny, most couples can't wait to have time to themselves...we relished in the time together, the walks we took and settling into our new world. We couldn't have a real Christmas with family, but we made the most of it, same for New Year's, alone together in the house, we did puzzles, ate "fun" food and brought 2021 in together. A better year, we said...after all, how could it get any worse?

2022, even though everything was starting to be "the new normal," Chris really struggled. The business was moving, and he knew he wouldn't fit the part in the new office as he didn't have the type of clientele to run his business. He was given the task of taking courses for a license he had never been interested in during his entire career. At the age of 63, he had some memory issues from a fall he had outside a Cineplex one icy evening.

He was attempting to wind down his career to retire on December 18, 2024, my 60th birthday. Instead, he was fighting to breathe as this transition was going to happen, and he couldn't find assistance to continue his business in another office as everyone was still working from home. He was crushed, and all he wanted to do was ensure his clients were well taken care of.

There was also the continuing issue of long-term care residents being in isolation, which meant fewer visits to his mom that he looked after; Markham isn't around the block. But the one thing he was looking forward to was his daughter, and our grandchildren were coming for Easter from England; we finally had a house so they could stay with us. We shopped for gifts, borrowed toys, and bought all of their favorite foods in anticipation of this long-awaited visit. Sadly, one of the passports did not arrive on time due to long delays, which meant their trip was cancelled. We were heart broken; returning as many items as we could and donating what we didn't need; except for the two special bunnies we had personalized. This I believe was the icing on the cake so to speak for Chris.

Chris continued to spiral; I did everything possible to help him. After all, we were a team. I suggested he bring his business home, and I would do all the administrative work or retire, and we would sell our home. We worked hard to get where we were "but always said we would live in a cardboard box if it meant we would be together. That's what love is all; sacrifice, and we were deeply in love with each other.

In April 2022, the dreaded virus finally caught up to us; I had it first and slept in the spare room. After five days, I no longer had to isolate, but then Chris caught it. He had to isolate himself from the world but not from me (it still baffles me). I went out for groceries and suffered an asthma attack while driving. I managed to call 911 and then Chris. He was frantic as he couldn't come to get me (yes, we listened to the rules); he contacted our friend who worked on the same street where I was. As I was placed on the stretcher and into the back of the ambulance, our friend took my car to his work and managed to get it to our home.

When I was released from the hospital hours later, Chris didn't care; he came to get me, and I was so happy he no longer cared what the "rules" were. He jumped out of the car, grabbed me into his arms, and cried because he felt bad that he couldn't do anything to help me during my crisis. He was never really the same after this, losing interest in things and sleeping too much, although the battle in his brain never really allowed him to rest.

Two weeks before Mother's Day weekend, Chris was very quiet; he was searching for answers and attempting to get help, but finding a therapist was very difficult, and EAP was no help. He went to see our family physician to discuss his anxiety and mental health, filled with dark moments. Other than being handed a prescription, no other help was offered;

just a statement that there was a two to three-year wait period for a therapist.

We walked to the pharmacy closest to home. He didn't want our pharmacist to know what was going on (the entire family were clients), and Chris was a proud person. Little did he realize that they would have stepped in, but when you are not dealing well mentally, you don't consider who might be able to help.

We received information from the pharmacist on side effects to watch for; he was terrified to take the medication but decided to try it. Of course, these medications are not miracle pills; it takes time to start working, something he didn't have. He continued to have frightening nightmares, and I held him close while he cried; everything he ever dreamed of was falling apart, and he didn't know how to stop it, nor did I other than being right there for him.

We started gardening on May 7th, 2022; the weather was gorgeous, so why not get started early? In the afternoon, we went golfing for our first round of the season; I had bought Chris a new push golf cart that he put together and was excited to use. He was still quiet but happy to golf with friends, be outdoors, and not think about anything else. He smiled; he laughed it was so nice to see. We had our typical pizza dinner, meat lovers for the girls and Hawaiian for the boys, and called it a night.

On Mother's Day, we opted not to drive to Markham; he wasn't up to it as he was very tired. I made plans to have brunch with a friend, which we did every year before the pandemic. I didn't pay attention to Chris asking me if I really had to go; I promised him I wouldn't be long, an hour and a bit at the most. He promised to stay off the computer and do some yard work that he really wanted to do.

Sadly, when I arrived home, he was working on the computer, something he did whenever he wasn't asleep. I made him turn it off, quickly got changed, and said let's go. He wasn't reluctant but was quiet again. He wanted to cook dinner for me; I'm an eat-once-a-day kind of girl, and he said it was okay; there was no need to. Another regret. Chris always treated me like a queen on Mother's Day. He wouldn't let me drive and always had a plan, but not this year. He had no plans other than I wasn't driving.

We decided on Gananoque, to escape from Kingston, and just be together. His driving was slightly erratic, and many times, he ended up in the middle of the road; I suggested the trail on Highway 15 with the motive of Tim Hortons being our first stop. He agreed, and I took the keys back when we arrived.

We walked the hidden trails, and he was exceptionally withdrawn. We held hands, he squeezed mine often and I finally said, "How do I reach you? I miss you and need you to talk to me." He cried; it broke my heart; he felt defeated, disappointed in himself, a failure. I listened intently until it was time to tell him how much I loved him, that I believed in him, and he wasn't a failure.

What I should have done was get him back in the car and drive to a hospital anywhere in Ontario; instead, he wanted to continue to walk downtown, and I agreed. We walked, poked our head into local shops (a past time of ours) and landed at the Iron Duke, one of many pubs we enjoyed, and the selling point was always the patio which was open! We quickly grabbed two seats outside, he played with dogs who were with their owners on the patio, chatted with friends we bumped into and seemed to be okay.

We discussed options moving forward and narrowed it down: bring the business home (there was a huge cost to buy his business back from the owner, which was part of his spiral) or retire, and we would sell our home.

It was a beautiful evening, and he wanted to put the patio tables together and take out the chairs; this was typically a May "24" weekend project, but that was also our 20th anniversary; our plan was to hide in Montreal at the hotel where we first met. We accomplished setting everything up and watched a movie together, his head on my lap, my hand rubbing his back; he fell asleep. I stayed there in one spot for what seemed like forever...when he woke up, we went to bed after closing everything up and his favorite bedtime pastime, giving multiple treats to his cat, Lefty. I held him close that night and truly thought we were going to be okay.

Monday, May 9th, 2022: On our typical morning, he would get up early (5 am) and go to the basement to work out watching one of his shows. He would always have to wake me up because I would turn around and ignore my alarm. He came to get me around 6 am to work out; he planned to do weights, I would do core, and the following day, we would switch. Because he was finished before me, he went to meditate and write in his journal something he had been doing for 9.5 years.

I finished my workout and headed for the shower because I was training new employees online at 9:30 am and I always made sure to be with Chris before he left in the morning. When I came out of the shower, he was very disappointed because he had missed it, yes, we still showered together even after all these years. After work we were going to continue with the garden, I promised we'd take one a shower together then; I just wanted to see him smile.

When it was time for him to get ready to leave, I walked with him to the kitchen and confirmed that he had his lunch, his swipe key, and his cell phone. I made him a coffee while he put on his black trench coat and fixed his collar like I always did. We chatted one more time about his decisions, and he promised to call me before noon.

I suggested driving him to work and waiting in the parking lot, canceling my training session; after all, I was the trainer, and I could do it. I suggested we run away together once he discussed his decision with his boss, and he said we would go on our anniversary. I held him close and told him how much I loved him, and he said he loved me so much that he was the luckiest man alive because I was always there for him.

I felt his defeat, though; after over 30 years in the business, it was ending but not the way it was planned. I opened the garage door for him and stood at the window, but instead of watching him leave that morning, I looked away, another regret because I might have noticed something. He left at 8:50 am as he always did, and I waited patiently for lunch time.

I didn't receive a call, but someone at my door at 11:35 am; a Police Officer stood in my doorway; he proceeded to tell me there had been a tragic accident and needed information from me.

Around the block from our home is an overpass to the train tracks, Chris jumped onto the oncoming train at 9:07 a.m; it was caught on a dash cam.

There would be no more calls. There would be no more. I love you. My life changed forever that day; I became a widow at the age of 57. I have a lot of regret for things I should have done and didn't do, and honestly, I will never forgive myself for not seeing how deep this truly was.

As the 2nd Anniversary gets closer, I am less stable. I am still numb. I continue to miss him more every day; I am in acute grief and very grateful to the true friends who have stuck by me. Many have walked away. I have been in therapy for almost two years now and will attend a bereavement group to see if it helps (with the encouragement of a close friend). I hide my feelings a lot now; people don't want to hear how much I miss Chris; most think I should move on; you don't move on when you lose your soulmate and best friend. When I smile, it's only a mask. I keep myself "busy," so people think if they only realize how much time I spend alone.

You try to navigate around grief as best as possible. There are days I can't get out of bed. There are days I can not stay home. I lost my life that day, our life; it's not the cardboard box and lifetime dream we had. I will never understand it; I would have given up everything to be with him. I know that when someone suicides, they are not aware of the consequences and loss they leave behind.

I have lost two out of three of his daughters (they blame me) and three young grandchildren. I have a great relationship with his youngest daughter and our only grandson; the problem is they live around the world.

There is so much more to our story; perhaps I will have an opportunity to share it in another chapter book.

I love you, Beastie, forever and always.

Your Beastmaster

xoxo

Tracey

"One word frees us of all the weight and pain of life:
that word is love."
Sophocles

6

A STORY OF HEALTH, HEARTBREAK AND HEALING: FACING LIFE'S UNPREDICTABLE CHALLENGES, ONE OBSTACLE AT A TIME

ASHLEY HILLARD

"We don't know how strong we are until being strong is the only choice we have."
Breast Cancer Awareness Campaign.

If you had told me that when I was just 21 years old, I would be over 500 pounds. I would have laughed in your face. But there I was, moving back to British Columbia after living in Alberta for six years. Upon my arrival, it was made clear to me that my appearance was not what was expected.

Over the next year, I lost about 100 pounds and stayed between 350 and 400 pounds. No matter what I ate or how hard I tried, the weight wouldn't go away.

Fast-forward to my 30s, when I met my now husband (who loves me unconditionally just the way I am), and I was in a career I thought would last my lifetime.

Within the next six years, my weight fluctuated. My best friend (ILU Tahna) introduced me to Weight Watchers, and at first, I was skeptical and hesitant. I didn't believe that talking about my feelings or facing myself in the mirror would do any good. I have never been so happy to be so very wrong.

At first, the weight came off easily, and then it didn't. I worked hard on my eating habits, eating lots of salads and proteins, etc. I went to the gym five to six days a week for two or more hours each time.

I would do an hour's workout, swim for an hour, hit the warm, relaxing therapy pool, go to the hot tub, shower, and go home. I LOVED it! I LOVED! How strong I felt, the energy I never had, and how I looked in the mirror. I paid for a trainer to help me with a program, and we met once a week. He made me work, and I couldn't get enough of it. He had to tell me several times to take a day off!

This was in 2019, the same year my then fiancé and I were planning on getting married. I bought the most beautiful dress second-hand, and it was a few sizes too small for me, so I used that as my motivation. I was going to fit in that dress!

In six months of hard work, I lost 90 pounds! I felt on top of the world, and I thought I had finally found what was going to help me lose weight and keep it off. I had such high hopes and dreams for my future: a future of not being fat and finally being in control of my life.

March 2020 is the month the world shuts down. In a matter of weeks, I lost the place I felt the most empowered (the gym/pool). My work closed for 73 days (about two and a half months), and I was stuck at home, not allowed to go anywhere. My fiancé still had to work, as he was an essential worker.

So, I was at home, alone, all day with nothing to do but watch TV and eat. At first, I tried to stick to the healthy foods we had been eating for the last while, and it was easy. Then I would see something to eat that I knew I shouldn't, but that voice inside would say, "Oh, come on, one isn't going to hurt you." No, one wouldn't, but when was one ever enough? Over the course of the next 73 days, I gained back 60 of the 90 pounds I had lost, and to this day, I still struggle to lose even five pounds.

Then came June 26th, 2021, "I'm so sorry to be the one who must tell you this, ma'am, but you have breast cancer." Those are words I never thought I would ever hear being said to me.

I had found a lump a year earlier but ignored it because I am a big girl; I got lumps and bumps, and I didn't think anything of it. After hearing those words, I didn't even get the chance to digest them before I had surgery to remove the tumor. It was all done within a few weeks, and it was hard. I felt so depressed and sad. Why me? Why did I develop breast cancer? I know I haven't always been good, but did I really deserve this?

Mass depression took over me, and all I did was sleep. I'd get up in the morning and pretend I was ok, but as soon as my husband left for work, I would sleep. I had nothing to do but watch TV and sleep. I tried to go for walks, but my body was just too tired from the chemo. I had no energy, and at the time, the world was still very much engulfed in the fight against COVID-19.

Believe what you will about it, but those vaccines helped to save my life. My oncologist told me, "If you get COVID-19 while undergoing chemo, you will most likely die. I won't be able to save you". That was not a scare tactic. She was trying to save my life. For those who do not know, when one is undergoing chemotherapy treatments, they have a ZERO immune system. A simple cold can kill them.

Now that I have completed the treatments almost two years ago, my body is different. I don't have the stamina I once had. I could not go as hard at the gym as I used to unless they wanted to peel me off the floor! I recently started swimming again. I try to go three days a week. It's helping with my mobility issues and decreasing the pain just a little, and I have tried hard to stick to a routine.

It was easy to do with just swimming. At first, I feared being judged because I had gained some weight, and my bathing suit didn't fit like it used to (nothing was hanging out; this fear of judgment is all in my head). When I put on my bathing suit for the first time in over a year, it fit well and covered what I wanted to cover. That first time getting in the pool after so long was magical. I felt like my body just remembered what to do, and just like that, I was at home in the pool once again. I got to enjoy this for a time, but it was a short one.

About six months ago, my legs started to do the most extraordinary thing, and they would cease to work for no reason. I started having spells where my legs would go numb, and I would fall—the first time scared the shit out of me. I was walking down my hallway, and suddenly, I wasn't. I was on the floor with no feeling in my legs. I mentioned it to my doctors, and it was sort of shrugged off as a post-chemo symptom and," It should go away."

Well, it hasn't. Slowly, over time, the falls became more frequent and serious. I fell in the shower and landed on the edge of the tub, half in and half out; because of that, I have a rib on my right side that is pushing inward and makes lying on my back very uncomfortable.

Other falls have resulted in bruises, twisted ankles, and pulled muscles in my back. The most recent fall was a trail walk with my husband on our ten-year anniversary. My legs went numb, and I tripped over a rock on the path. I fell hard on the pavement and ended up spraining my wrist and bruising my whole right side.

On April 11th, I had my six-month check-in with my oncologist. I told her that the falls were still problematic and that they were more frequent. This time, she was concerned and ordered CT scans, MRIs, and a body scan. She is concerned that something is pressing on my spine, causing my legs to lose all feeling and function.

As a result of the chemotherapy, I have two degenerative vertebrae in my lower spine. This is where she believes the problem is. She said there were two options right now, without any of the tests done: 1) A surgery that could leave me paralyzed or 2) Manage it with medications and injections but live with the potential of any one of the future falls could leave me paralyzed.

I said I didn't like those options and needed a third one. She said that there isn't a third one at this time, without seeing any of the scans/tests. Then she said that it could be a tumor pressing on my spine; I told her that was not an acceptable option, and I refused to think that.

But I have thought about it often. It's always just off to the side in my mind. The fear of being paralyzed terrifies me. Not that I am a star athlete or anything (the farthest thing from it!), but the fears are just as real for me. The thought of not being able to walk again...having that always in my mind is the kind of thought that keeps me up at night, and why I smoke so much weed at night. I'm just trying to numb myself enough to sleep.

Sometimes, I am successful; other nights, I am not. I asked my GP for something to help me sleep, so I've now added medication to help me sleep to my daily regimen of pills. And it helps to keep me asleep once I am there, but getting there is the issue. I feel tired during the day, but come night/bedtime, I'm wide awake. It is an ongoing battle.

But for now, we wait. Thankfully, because of the urgency my oncologist put on these tests, they are all happening within the next three weeks. I have a CT scan today and then the body scan on Monday. Unfortunately, that means missing two days of my schooling, but I must put myself first. I need to remember that I am the most important thing in my life because there is no life without me! I must put my health before anything and everyone.

Ever since cancer, I have had a completely different outlook on life. Before, I put everyone and everything before myself, and now, no. I come first, and I must put myself first; no one else is going to do it in my place, so I must.

With the new concerns that have now been realized, I am back to not being allowed to do the things that I enjoy. No more gym, swimming, walks etc. Just until my doctors have the results from all the scans and tests, we will find out what this is and how to proceed.

I was so angry the rest of that day and the days following. No, I was pissed. Thoughts like, "Seriously?!? Was the cancer not enough?" "Why ME?" "It's not fucking fair!" I felt defeated. Like no matter what I do, I just cannot win. Life has handed me so much shit, and I know the old saying that we are never given more than we can handle but ENOUGH already.

I've always been forced to be tough, to be strong. Well, I'm tired of being strong. I don't want to keep fighting the residual effects of the chemo treatments. I just want to finish school, find a great job, and finally feel like I belong somewhere.

I thought I had that with my career as an E.C.E. for 12 years, but after losing my job while battling cancer and the few centers I worked at after the treatments were done, my body cannot do that job anymore. It was sad to realize that I could no longer do the job I loved. It was a few days of mourning that loss for me before I realized that it was a blessing in disguise.

Now, I am on the path to an amazing new career as a counselor. That is something I have always thought of doing. I am almost done with year one of two of school and love it. Through my schooling, I have learned so many things about myself and have become firmer in what I will and will not tolerate in my life. I have met some fantastic people and formed a few close bonds with some classmates (Shout out to Alyssa, ILU).

When first being interviewed for school, I was asked, "Why do you want to become a counselor?" I answered, "I want to be that person for someone I needed and didn't have." And if I can help just one person who is going through something, then I feel like my life will have meaning. I know I did not survive three suicide attempts, poverty, homelessness, and breast cancer for nothing. I am here for a reason other than to find my fishie- my husband Jim (ILU). I believe I was put through all of that for what my life has become today. There must be a reason I am still here when so many others are not (RIP Greg). I have always known that I was a "helper" in more ways than one. Becoming a counselor is one of those ways.

Sometimes, I just sit outside on my bench and listen to owls hooting in the trees, the frogs singing their melodies off in the distance, and breathing in the cool night air. Being outside makes me feel so at peace. I love being by the water, but I feel the most at home and peaceful when I am surrounded by forest. There is just something about being surrounded by huge, old trees, breathing in the fresh air, and listening to the natural world around me. It helps me to ground myself and brings me an appreciation for all the life around me and the life within me. I believe I need to be in the forest more often to help ground me and bring me peace.

Luckily, I live on Vancouver Island, and I am always surrounded by big, beautiful forests.

(Upon finishing writing this, I received word from my doctor that the CT scan came back clear, so that is good news! One test down, three to go. I hope that one of them yields some results or at least points us in the right direction of what to do about the falls.)

"Turn your wounds into wisdom."
Oprah Winfrey

7

_____

FINDING MY INNER LIGHT AGAIN: ECHOES OF LOVE

CATHERINE CHAPMAN-KING

"New beginnings are often disguised as painful endings."
Laozi

A sense of contentment washed over me as I returned from a peaceful weekend getaway. Little did I know that the solace I had just experienced would soon be shattered by a life-altering phone call.

The message left for me was urgent—"Call your family immediately." My heart raced as I dialed the number, a sense of foreboding settling in the pit of my stomach. At that moment, as I listened to the words that spilled from my daughter's mouth at the other end of the line, my world came crashing down. Things would never be the same.

My husband, Dimitri, had been found lifeless by one of our other children, our second youngest son. The weight of the news was unbearable, as if my bones had turned to liquid, causing me to collapse onto the floor, when I heard this horrific news. In that instant, darkness enveloped me, suffocating the light that once illuminated my days. I felt so lost, questioning if this was real or a bad nightmare; this couldn't really be happening.

My entire body trembled, shaking in total disbelief. This can't be true. The absolute shock of hearing this reality was too much to process and absorb, so it affected my physical being; I went numb.

You need to understand that this man was the center of my world. I had been with him for more than half my life. We went through the good, the bad, and the ugly together. We had rough patches, of course, but he loved me, and I loved him. He was my best friend. I wasn't there—I wasn't there for him—is all I could think.

My husband, Dimitri, had a work injury about a year and a half prior to his passing. He worked outdoors and absolutely loved going to work. He loved his job he loved providing for his family, but he tore his ACL at work and required surgery. It was quite a long healing process, and he was in a great deal of pain. Of course, the doctors would prescribe pain medicine and painkillers that eventually took more control over him.

It was during this time that things became difficult; he spiraled down into depression, sitting at home, not working. He would have mood swings from the pain that he was in or if the painkillers started wearing off him, and we had our arguments. I felt like the pain medication and the drugs were taking more control over his life. I saw it as self-destructive at this point, and I made a decision to separate temporarily.

It was not long after that that he accidentally overdosed. That might shed some light into the background and also why I carried a lot of guilt for a very long time after his passing.

There were so many dark days that turned into weeks, and those weeks turned into months, and I found myself trapped in this void where absolutely no light seemed to penetrate. It was so dark.

The struggle to find the will to continue living became a daily battle for me. I'd wake up in the mornings so angry. Why did I wake up? Why am I here? What's my purpose? I didn't want to be here anymore. It was too heavy to wake up to this horrific reality.

Here I am, grieving, and I was expected to deal with what life throws at me and continue with my daily responsibilities as a mother. I couldn't do it; my children needed me, and here I felt like I had nothing else to give; I felt lifeless inside, so very empty.

Looking back at this experience, the hardest part of forgiving myself is the fact that my children needed me the most through this horrific and heart-wrenching time with the loss of their father, and I couldn't give them what they needed; I was completely broken. I was always the SUPERWOMEN in my family, the strong-willed, disciplined, and UNBREAK-

ABLE Mum. I was the one who always knew what to do, and this time, I didn't; I had no clue what to do.

The loss of my husband had a profound impact on our entire family, like an exploding bomb sending shrapnel flying in every direction. It was incredibly difficult to cope. I not only lost my husband but also his income. The world did not stop moving, and bills continued to come in. I felt depressed and overwhelmed with all of these responsibilities, especially with my children depending on me. It was not easy. There were moments when I would gaze up at the sky and cry, "Why did you leave me to face all of this alone? Why?"

For the first time, I was alone to face this world, and it was scary. Within me someway, somehow, a tiny spark remained, fueled by the love I held for our five beautiful children - my pillars of strength, now in their teenage and early twenties.

With my three boys still at home, their presence was a constant reminder that life still carried on. I was also reminded because one of my neighbor's children would come by to show her love and check up on me. She knew I was struggling with depression. She'd come by daily to post pictures of my entire family and friends on my bedroom wall. She made a mural of love. She said that she did this because every day, when I opened my eyes, she wanted me to see all the people who love me to give me the strength to carry on in life. I will never forget her act of love and kindness. That act of love I think about to this day warm-heartedly.

Another act of kindness and love I hold dear to my heart during this time was from a neighboring family. They brought us huge home-cooked meals made with love from their family to ours. They'd bring an abundance of food like basmati rice, tandoori chicken, samosas, and more. They did this for about a week straight after my husband had passed. They provided what I couldn't during this debilitating time of grief for my children and myself. I will forever be grateful for what they did.

Acts of love and kindness like these have started to renew my faith in humanity truly. I really had isolated myself during this time. I was so deep in my head, Just trying to forget what was going on in the environment around me. I never went out anymore. I used to get together with my friends all of the time. We'd get together on birthdays and go camping. Even though we were busy with our own lives, we managed to find time to get together on different occasions throughout the years.

I do have a small, close circle of friends that I have known since grade school. I hadn't seen anyone or gotten together with anyone for about a year now, already passed. It was last summer. Dimitri had passed at this point, and I had been a hermit, just completely anti-social.

A few of my good friends, as amazing as they are we've been through so much together over the years, knowing one another for so long. They spontaneously showed up at my doorstep this summer, and they literally just grabbed me, told me to pack a bag and kidnap me, so to speak, and took me away to go camping like we used to do all the time. They would not take no for an answer. I love them so much for doing this. They knew what I needed. I needed a good kick in the butt and brought back to reality.

Looking back, I think it was during this time that I cracked a smile again; I actually laughed and felt alive for a second, being away in the outdoors with my beloved girlfriends. I had been in my head for so long, constantly thinking and analyzing my life in general. I just needed to get out of my head and back to living.

It was then that I began to change my perspective. Gratitude seeped into my soul, and I learned to appreciate the beauty in every passing moment. I embraced the fragility of life, understanding that once a moment passed, it could never be reclaimed. I began to look through those eyes of gratitude and felt so thankful for the time, experience, and years I had with my husband. I was grateful for his love, to find a love like that, and the time we had together for the time we did. So many people in this world may never get to experience that kind of love or connection at all, so I was blessed. I was so grateful for our beautiful, precious children.

I slowly began to feel less sadness within my soul and started to feel lighter. I would think about my life with Dimitri and certain moments we shared over so many years, and yes, it would still bring a tear to my eye, but I'd smile now. I feel warm inside, filled with love instead of the dark emptiness I had felt for so long.

With each breath I took, I slowly found the strength to be out of my head and more present in my daily life. I learned to lead with love, to cherish the time we had together as a family, and to honor the memory of my beloved husband. It also taught me to love harder and hold my children closer every day. I stopped worrying about the small stuff and started to see what truly mattered in this world.

My once heavy heart started to lighten. I discovered solace in the smallest of things—a gentle breeze on my skin, the birds chirping in the morning, the smell of a campfire, the stillness of the lake, the warm sunshine on my face, the laughter of my children, and the warmth of a shared home-cooked meal.

I realized that life, despite its hardships, was meant to be enjoyed not suffered, and that it's okay to not be okay in a sense. If I see my life as a book, well, then the part of it I shared with Dimitri was a chapter in my life I'll forever cherish, but I need to move on to these next chapters in my life, and I see now that I can create any story I want. I now wake up looking forward to the day ahead and what it might bring.

Life is a precious gift that is here for joy. If we could all just lead with love, this world would truly be a better place to live in. We humans often complicate our lives with worries, fears, and endless drives. We chase success and material gain, Forgetting that families and love should always reign. That's what matters in this life we have.

With my newfound determination within, I've made a conscious effort to be kind to everyone I encounter. When

Dimitri passed away, some of the things that played over in my head were the arguments and fights we had, mean things that were said out of anger, and all the petty little things that we had arguments over. It killed me inside to think about it.

I carried huge guilt. I understood that each person carried their own burdens, their own silent battles, as we all do. I didn't see all the beautiful blessings I had in my life as pure as I do now, and so I want to spread compassion like wildfire, knowing that a simple act of kindness could be the light someone desperately needs in their life, just like I needed when I lost my husband.

Anger was a heavy burden I had carried for far too long in my life, and slowly, it began to dissipate. In time, I started to forgive not only others but myself as well. That's probably the hardest part: learning to love and forgive yourself.

We all go through the emotional rollercoaster after the loss of a loved one; there's the turbulent ride of blame, then that long guilt trip, of course, the heated ride of anger, then sadness; it's quite the ride. I can tell you I definitely wasn't prepared for it. My advice is to strap on a helmet and hang on for dear life.

Some of what I experienced in my ride was that it could've changed the outcome if I had done this or that. What if I hadn't gone away that weekend? What if I was home? What if I answered previous phone calls? It was never-ending. What if?

I think it was when we had to bury Dimitri, my late husband, that my brother wanted to talk with me in the midst of my dark grief. I could barely think or function, and my brother proceeded to tell me this tale of a boy who went to the ice cream parlor; he had a choice of strawberry, chocolate, or Vanilla Ice cream.

Now my brother turns to me and asks me to pick a flavor; I'm thinking to myself, here I am today, I am burying my husband, and my brother's telling me a stupid story about a boy and wanting me to pick a flavor of ice cream I don't get the point of this. I was agitated. My brother could see this in me, and he just told me to pick a flavor, any flavor, just say it, and that there was a point to his story.

So I shout out chocolate! Okay, I pick chocolate, holy. Now my brother ask me why did I pick chocolate?

Seriously? I'm over this story he has to tell at this point. So I shouted out again," I chose it because I chose it, okay, that's it."

My brother then said to me, "That's right, Cat. It was your choice; just like in this life, we all have choices, and some of those choices have benefits, and others have consequences." It was at this moment that I completely realized his point.

My husband made choices during the last days of his life that resulted in his own death. My husband, whom we initially thought took his life, we later found out from the toxicology report that it was an accidental overdose that caused respiratory depression; he laid down and just went to sleep and never woke up.

My brother's ultimate point was that we all have choices to make in life, and some of the choices that my husband made resulted in his death, and those were his choices with his consequences. They were not my choices; I was not responsible for his ultimate demise.

This gave some clarity to my clouded emotions and thoughts; it gave me some perspective.

I've started to learn the power of letting go, releasing the weight that had held me down for so very long. This was not an easy task, but I just put one foot in front of the other and took a step forward every day. That's all I could do.

Love, so unexpected and beautiful, found its way back into my life. Years after my husband's passing, I met a man named Jamal at a mutual friend's birthday party. Honestly, the last thing I wanted was a love connection or another relationship. I was still healing from the loss of my husband, Dimitri, whom I had spent more than half my life with, even though I was still young.

In ways, I feel Dimitri sent Jamal to me, knowing what kind of person I need in my life. The night we met at my friend's birthday party, we just connected. There was something about him that intrigued me, wanting to know more. It was like our minds and our souls just had an immediate connection. This man was different, and I was interested.

I have held onto the memories of my past, and that's okay. We are here to make memories, and there are so many beautiful memories I'll never forget. I will always love Dimitri, but now

I've embraced the present with a fervor I have never known before. I've made a vow to myself to love others and myself fiercely, cherish every connection in my life, and live unapologetically from this day forward.

I have learned that it's okay to stumble along the path of grief. You need to walk through it to overcome it and deal with that reality. In doing so, I discovered the resilience of the human spirit, of my spirit, and the capacity to heal within. I've been able to find joy once again in this life. And I've learned that it's okay for me to be happy again without carrying guilt.

In the end, my journey taught me that life is too short to waste on negativity and regret. " What you can do today, you should not put off until tomorrow," my Mum would always say growing up, and now I get it. I choose to live every day fully now, to seize each precious moment that life gives me.

Deep down, I know that Dimitri is still looking down around me in spirit. The only thing that he ever wanted when he was alive was to see me smile, and I know that's all he still wants for me and our children to be happy. I know this for a fact!

I went through something that was an extremely freaky and fascinating experience that gave me a certain sense of closure. I met the new love of my life, Jamal, about three years after my husband's passing.

About two years into our relationship, we were making a big move from the city to the country. I really needed to get away from the chaos of the city because my environment really affected me, and I found more serenity Being around nature, animals, and water rather than cars, traffic, and chaos with lots of people.

We had just moved into our home in the country. And it was this one night we were just relaxing. I was kind of falling asleep on the couch; I looked up. Jamal had this look on his face, almost as if he had seen a ghost, and I asked him, "What was wrong? Are you okay? He just looked like he was almost in a trance. He told me He was okay, but there was a man in his head.

He explained to me that he could see what he looked like, and it was almost as if he was talking in his ear. He just looked like he was in a trance, and he said to me he was okay but that there was a man in his head. He explained to me that he could see what he looked like, and it was almost as if he was talking in his ear.

I will let you know at this point: when I met my new love, Jamal, I never really talked about my husband's passing and how he passed the details. I never showed him a picture of what he looked like or got into all of that.

So I asked Jamal what this man looked like. "Can you describe what he looks like?" So he started to describe what the man who was talking to him looked like in his head. And from the description, it started to sound like my husband Dimitri. So, at this point, I'm freaked out. Jamals already freaked out because he's kind of like, what the heck is going on, like what's happening right now?

So I pulled out a picture of Dimitri, and I showed it to him, and the second I showed it to him, his eyes widened, and his face lit up, and he was like, that's the man that is the man that is in my head right now talking to me.

So, as we are going through this completely freaky experience, Jamal is telling me what this man, my husband, who has passed Dimitri, is saying in his head. He was talking about the night he passed. All he kept saying was how sorry he was sorry, sorry for this happening, sorry for this happening, sorry for leaving me with all the children to deal with life to tell his mom sorry. He talked about other details of his night and expressed that he did not mean for it to happen. He also continued to tell my guy to watch over me and the children that he was glad that I was happy again because he wants me to be happy.

He also told him to tell me that he loves me and that I know what to do.

Jamal looked at me, and he didn't understand what he meant when he said you know what to do. I explained to him that during our lives raising a family, Dimitri always said to me that I knew what to do in any situation. It was amazing.

To me, this experience was not only fascinating and something we could both not explain, but it also really warmed my heart and gave me a certain sense of closure.

I remember before Dimitri even passed, we used to talk about death and dying, what we would want, etcetera. It was always an uncomfortable situation, but we would have the conversations, and he'd always say that there was a way he would find to come back and let me know that he was okay on the other side.

I've also realized that there is a whole world out there to experience. We have complete and total control over our thoughts and what we can create as our reality; it's like a blank canvas, and you are the artist able to paint any picture that you want. Anything that we want in this lifetime is waiting right there at the tip of our fingertips, just waiting for us to reach out and grab it to try and believe.

I realize that we all need to find happiness within ourselves first and foremost. It is our responsibility to do so. We can not have happiness depending on other people or things. It needs to be something that you find deep within yourself, and that doesn't mean that you have everything you want in life, but it does mean that you're happy with what you do have in your life and that you appreciate everything and everyone around you and do not take any of that for granted.

I once thought I'd never see the light in this life again, but I felt like I had been drifting away for many years. Now, I found the light within myself again; that fire burns inside me and warms my heart, and I feel it finally beat again. I'm happy to wake up every day now and look forward to that uncertainty of what's to come. There was definitely a beacon of hope that illuminated the darkest corners of my soul and brought me back to life, and I'm grateful for everything.

I found myself again, my inner light shining brightly from within. I smile and embrace what Dimitri and I created, which still lives on in five beautiful children and nine precious grandchildren.

I look up to the sky from time to time, smile, and thank him. I tell him to look at the life we created together out of love. Thank you for that love that will always live on. We will always have that. I'm so grateful.

"You never know how strong you are until being strong is your only choice."
Bob Marley

8

WALKING THE RAZOR'S EDGE: HOW PLACING ONE FOOT IN FRONT OF THE OTHER GETS US THROUGH THE HARD MESSY TIMES

LISA FAIRNEY

"I find that it's best to take one step at a time and cross each bridge as they come to you."
Michael Stuhlbarg

Advice from my amazing Gigi Edwards

"Edwards' don't Quit! Pull yourself up by the bootstraps and get on with it".

Have you ever had one of those feelings like something terrible was about to happen?

Some may call it a premonition, a vision, or an intuitive knowing; this wisdom that somehow extends beyond what your mind can comprehend, but deep in your gut you just know there's truth to it? In the depth of receiving it, it feels like a calm knowing, like a sure thing, despite whatever crazy content exists within it?

I remember it vividly:

I was laying on my bed, wrestling with myself and my emotions, feeling overwhelmed with my life and whether I was up to the task of taking it on. At this point, I was no stranger to hard things: I was in the middle of a divorce with an abusive ex-husband that I had two young children with, and after having to live at my parent's house and find somewhere to start a new life for me and my children, I was attempting to finish school on top of everything, so I could have a shot at a career and provide a better life and stable foundation for my girls. On this particular day, I was overwhelmed and at my wit's end, ready to give up. My feet felt heavy, my heart exhausted.

Can I really manage all of this on my own? How much longer would this take?

I was feeling suffocated by life. It felt like all my life choices were beginning to collapse on top of me. I failed once, so who's to say that won't happen again? The fear of the future and whether I was capable of achieving what I set out to do was attempting to find root in my mind.

Was I ever going to be a good enough and stable mother?

Was I ever going to finish school, let alone be healthy and present enough to raise my daughters well?

How would I balance it all?

In the midst of my psychological storm, that's when it happened. The sound of a razor buzzing flooded my awareness, and I saw these delicate, blond pieces of hair falling like feathers to the ground. I snapped out of the vision. And pleaded to know, who's hair was that? Was it mine?

I brushed it off, thinking that maybe, due to everything I just went through, my fear was getting the best of me. You know that thing we like to do where we project that the other shoe will have to drop at some point soon? I was notorious for that.

What I didn't know was that this vision was the beginning of a really hard period in my life that took me to the depths of my strength and woke me up to a reality that would not only colour my life and my children's for the rest of their lives but would also be the pinnacle of an experience that built my character and set the course to make it through the many tough days ahead.

It was the fall in early November of 1986, many months after I received that vision. I was still attending school full-time and trying to find the balance of it all. Melissa, my oldest child, had been complaining of headaches on and off for nine weeks now. I had taken her to the doctors multiple times prior to this day, and they attributed her headaches to the "stress" that was happening in our household and family life.

I remember them explaining that children undergo stress when their environments change. And, of course, this was plausible: we had just moved to a new house, and I did get sick and was hospitalized with a pretty serious life-threatening illness a few months prior to this, but everything was good again, and we were back up and running as a family.

Something didn't feel right, but who am I to question a doctor? I thought. I didn't have any medical knowledge or background, but I couldn't get around this deep gut instinct that something was wrong. I didn't trust myself enough to listen to that instinct at the time. It wasn't until this one day Melissa was sitting on the living room floor and began to bang her head on the ground, crying: "Mommy. Mommy, it hurts. Help".

I rushed over to her to see that she wasn't in immediate physical danger and, in a panic, called the doctor. The doctor said that it sounded like she was having a temper tantrum and that everything was probably fine, and that there was no need to seek immediate medical attention.

Realizing I wasn't going to get anywhere with this doctor and finally having the courage to listen to my gut, I packed Melissa up and took her to the emergency room in our local town. After they didn't seem too impressed with our concerns, I decided to drive Melissa one and a half hours to the Children's Hospital in the main city to receive care. Why would my daughter be banging her head on the ground and be complaining of pain? She didn't have any other behavioural problems and was a sweet little girl. It all didn't make sense. I was invested in getting to the bottom of it.

When we got to the emergency department, they ran all of the same tests our local hospital did, but this time, they did a

CT scan of Melissa's head. After the CT scan, I remember the nurse coming in and asking if she could take Melissa on a walk while we waited. I thought it was an odd thing to ask.

I looked up at the nurse and asked, "Is the doctor coming to speak with us?" The nurse replied, "Yes, and I think it's best if Melissa is out of the room while we do so."

My heart sank into my gut; I felt my throat tightening as I swallowed as if I knew the weight of the news he was about to have me ingest. Surely, this can't be a good thing.

The doctor entered:

"Hi, I'm Dr. Stuhlbarg. I am the head of Pediatric Neuro-surgery. You must be Lisa, Melissa's Mom." he said graciously. "Please, sit down."

With my heart racing and no sense of my limbs and bodily function, I somehow found the edge of the bed. The moment I touched the bed, I began to sob and scream. I knew, and I could just sense, this doctor was about to deliver me the most devastating news I've received in my life. I composed myself just enough for the doctor to tell me what was happening. And I will tell you, the other shoe did drop.

"Lisa, I regrettably need to tell you that your daughter Melissa has a brain tumor. And due to its location, we are unsure at this time if it's operable." Dr Stuhlbarg took a breath, looking at me to see if I was ready to receive more; I slowly nodded, and with the thought that my daughter might die, I pressed on and asked him what this meant.

"Melissa's brain tumor is the size of a large plum, which is why she has been experiencing headaches from the built-up pressure in her skull; with her brain tissue having nowhere to go, if the tumor keeps growing, it may cause her to have seizures if we don't act soon. We fear that the tumor has grown into a location that removal at this time would mean possible ocular and cognitive deficits for Melissa going forward."

My face was blank, my heart palpitating, and my hands sweating; the first thought that ran across my mind was, "Is my daughter going to die?"

He continued on telling us that even though they weren't sure if they were going to be able to remove the tumor with surgery because of its location, due to the pressure building up in Melissa's head and the risk of seizures, they wanted to do a surgery to place a temporary shunt; and while they were in there, they would biopsy the tumor and check its location for the possibility of removal.

The doctor must have seen the look on my face or sensed my mind racing to one of the most terrible outcomes because before I could even manage to form words, he said, "I know this is a lot to process, so try to cross one bridge at a time." I sheepishly nodded.

He adds, "Oh, and don't go down the what if lane". I gulped and replied: Thank you.

Trying to stop my mind from racing down all the possible what if lanes, I took a deep breath and asked, "When will her surgery happen?"

He said: "She is first on the slate for tomorrow morning. You will stay here overnight for monitoring, and she will be prepared for the OR by 6 am."

I never thought at 24 years old, I'd be sitting on the edge of a bed in a hospital room receiving news that my five-year-old daughter had a brain tumor that I'd find out later; they didn't have the technology or innovation yet to safely surgically remove.

I felt so hopeless. I wanted to buckle under the weight of the circumstances. I didn't want to deal with what was happening. I didn't want to be so vulnerable to the unknown; I wanted to wrap my baby up in a blanket and run, but there it undeniably was, my next life challenge staring me straight in the face. I knew I needed to be strong for Melissa. I knew I needed to put one foot in front of the other and keep walking no matter how scared. There was no way out of this one. Only through.

On the morning of her surgery, I was a wreck on the inside, but I somehow pulled myself together, choked back my fears of her dying on the operating table, and gave my daughter a big hug to reassure her as they came to take her for surgery. She cried as they wheeled her away, Melissa not wanting to leave my side. With my mother holding me tight, I stood strong and tall as long as I could until I fell over onto the cold, hard floor, sobbing once Melissa was out of sight.

I sat there for what felt like days, feeling hopeless and like a failure — she was my daughter, I was supposed to take care of her, and this is the one time in my life where I simply couldn't. Everything was outside my control, so in the depth of my surrender, I began to pray. I pleaded that she would be okay, that she would be treated well and comforted.

As the hours went by, many nurses were walking in and out of the operating area. Many of them I asked for updates who had no idea what or whom I was talking about until one of the nurses finally came up to me with a brown paper bag. I gulped as she said, "Lisa, we thought you might want to have this."

I took the bag from the nurse, as she looked at me sympathetically. With the desire to forebode reality, I hesitantly opened the bag to see my daughter's beautiful, blond, feather-like hair inside.

There it was. Chills rolled down my spine. The vision I had months before just came full circle.

I looked up with tears in my eyes and asked the nurse: "What's happening in there? Is she doing okay?" The nurse smiled and said, "She's doing as well as can be expected at this point. It's going to be hours before we have any answers for you."

Hours? I thought to myself. How could I wait for hours?

Thankfully, my Mom saw that I was struggling to wrap my head around having no answers, and she encouraged me to get up, stretch my legs, and go for a walk. As I paced the halls of the children's hospital with my brown paper bag of Melissa's hair, stewing in my own worries and anxieties, I remember looking to my Mom and telling her, "I can't do this — I need to quit school and take care of her."

I was trembling and full of fear of what our family's future would hold until my Mom grabbed me by my arms, turned me towards her, and with her words somehow shook the sense back into me:

"Lisa — Edwards, don't quit! Pull yourself up by the bootstraps and get on with it."

I collapsed into my mom's arms, crying, feeling that I had met the edge of defeat. She was right. I had another daughter at home to think about, and I was already devoted to making a better life for all of us. Then I realized I was doing that thing that the doctor told me not to do — crossing the "what if" bridges before they came and making big decisions from a place of fear instead of from the circumstances. It felt like the only control I had in that moment.

Seven and half hours later, I finally received word that Melissa made it out of surgery and was in the ICU; they had her heavily sedated because of all the tubes, wires, and monitoring she needed with the shunt placement. The surgeon met me and my mom in a waiting room outside the ICU and explained.

"Fortunately, we were able to place a shunt and release some of the pressure building up in Melissa's skull, but the tumor is wrapped around her optic nerves and is in a tricky location; if we were to remove it, it could damage not only her vision but potentially her cognition. Unfortunately, it's inoperable at this time." My heart sank. "So what now? Can I see her?" I demanded.

The doctor explained that they would have to monitor her in the ICU for intracranial bleeding and make sure the shunt was working, and she would need to heal from the surgery. Only from there can we make a plan for what's next. The shunt was only decreasing the pressure related to brain fluid but couldn't account for the pressure from the tumor, nor if the tumor keeps growing. It was only a temporary solution.

As I walked in through the double doors of the intensive care unit, I stopped and took a deep breath as I approached her bed number. There was my baby: laying in a bed, her head wrapped in gauze, tubes, and wires everywhere, monitors and alarms beeping, and nurses moving cautiously and quickly around her bedside. I felt helpless at the state she was in.

A part of me was at ease I didn't have to see her bald head underneath all the bandages and face the reality of her bald head just yet. I went to her bedside, and the nurse gave me permission to only slightly touch her when I really wanted to wrap her in my arms and cry, but for the sake of not over stimulating her brain and all the critical tubes she had in place, I gently touched her hand and said, "It's going to be okay, sweetie. Mommy is here."

Melissa did well initially; the drain seemed to work in the interim, but as Dr. Stuhlbarg said, "It wasn't a forever solution." I kept catching myself going down all these roads of doubts and worries. Was my baby going to be like this forever? Would we ever get home? What's next? I knew my other daughter wasn't coping well with all the changes that were happening either.

Then, Melissa started having headaches again. The pressure began to build up in her brain, and we worried she might have a seizure soon due to all the stress her brain has gone through, surgery included. After a lot of meetings and discussions with oncologists, neurologists, neurosurgeons, and ophthalmologists, we decided the best course of treatment would be attempting radiation to shrink the tumor, which unfortunately would have some side effects we wouldn't quite know fully of until later on.

"What if it doesn't work?" I somehow got up the courage to ask.

The doctor looked at me compassionately and reminded me, "Let's cross that bridge if we come to it, Lisa. This is the safest option for now, in my opinion."

It's not easy to receive news that your five-year-old was going to undergo radiation on her brain, and yet, it felt like our only option without causing severe life-altering damage to her brain, so what other choice did I have? Death? Why was this my choice? My mother's words rang in the background of my brain, "Edwards' don't give up." So, with much hesitation and resistance, I said yes to the radiation treatment plan.

Here I was, a 24-year-old single mother with two children; one with a life-threatening illness, on the brink of a seizure with an inoperable tumor and about to undergo radiation, all the while in the midst of an entire lifestyle change, and trying to put myself through school. Was I up for it?

Honestly, if it weren't for the support of my parents and my Mother's words that day, I don't think I would have made it through the course of all that was expected of me, all the decisions I had to make through that process and even after this event.

When Melissa started radiation, it started with some complications before we saw the benefits. She ended up having multiple seizures, but surprisingly, it was because the tumor began to shrink — and fast. Too fast. I had to remind myself despite a little setback, that's what we were hoping for. Melissa finally became somewhat stable, and we were able to go to outpatient radiation treatment.

Things began to normalize again, I mean as normal as things could be with a chronically sick child, so I decided to keep pursuing my dreams and return to school. Upon arriving at school, one of my instructors pulled me into her office and said, "Lisa, I think you should quit school. It's only going to get harder, and I don't think you're going to make it with everything on your plate."

I was taken aback; that was not the conversation I was

expecting. At first, I was in shock, feeling the disbelief that this instructor cast upon me; was she right? Was I going to fail? I snapped out of my doubt, and the first thought that crossed my mind was: this may be hard, and I may have a lot to catch up on, but I can't give up now. Just like Melissa's treatment, I'm going to cross each bridge as it comes because I know if I was capable of that, I am capable of this, too. Then, I felt the fire in my belly rise up, and in the most confident breath of words, I said, "Edwards' don't quit." With a sincere smile, I followed it up with, "Thank you for giving me the encouragement to prove you wrong," and walked off and continued on despite the doubts about my finishing.

Not only did I manage to finish school, but I finished with honors and won an award for my efforts. The biggest win: I was able to provide a stable home for my daughters and move on from what felt like a dark, never-ending spiral of things happening to us. The sweet light at the end of the tunnel was that I met a generous man who looked after my kids as his own and supported me through rebuilding my life.

Melissa ended up receiving 30 radiation treatments to effectively treat the tumor, and I'd be lying if I said it didn't come without some bumps in the road that have required my family and me to be on a long walk with chronic illness and mental health issues that stemmed from her radiation and childhood experience, but Melissa is alive and overcame it all.

Life is difficult at times, and although we may not get to choose our circumstances, I've learned that it's what we do with them and how we work with what we are given that propels us into the best possible reality.

I'll never forget the words that the doctor had spoken to me in some of the scariest times with Melissa, to take one bridge at a time and not to get ahead of myself — and now I see that can be taken for the good things too. If we constantly fear the future and what's around the corner waiting for us, we won't appreciate the now. We may miss the blessings and gifts that life is trying to give us presently because we're too busy trying to react to life instead of responding to it.

When life feels chaotic and like I'm in the eye of a storm, I use these words to remind myself to slow down and be present in the moment; that our fears and doubts cause so much unnecessary worrying and can lead us down paths that aren't going to serve us in the long term.

No matter what has happened before, we have to not let fear drive us, or keep us from fully living — rather remembering that when life throws challenges at us, we are capable of rising to the occasion. At a time when I felt my weakest, I became my strongest by putting one foot in front of the other and walking the razor's edge, where the only way was through.

"New beginnings are often disguised as painful endings."
Lao Tzu

9

THE COURAGE TO HEAL: A LIFE REBUILT ON RESILIENCE

LOUISA THIESSEN

"True healing demands courage—the courage to face the past, the strength to embrace the present, and the resilience to build a future unshadowed by pain. This journey isn't about erasing old wounds; it's about transforming them into sources of power and wisdom." Louisa Thiessen

Imagine fleeing, thinking that you finally made your dream come true. You started a new life, and you were on your way to living happily ever after when, all of a sudden, you get the urge to drive your car into a ditch and end your life. The joy, pride, and curiosity you felt are replaced by despair and desperation. This feeling, as dark and fleeting as it might be, is exactly where my journey to healing began.

To understand the depth of this despair, you must understand where my story starts: in the bustling streets of Brooklyn, New York. Brooklyn was my world, a place of distinct contrasts where the sense of community was as palpable as the ever-present danger. The sound of children's laughter mingled with the sirens, and the smell of street food filled the air, alongside the tension of unseen threats. It was a place where every alleyway told a story, and every face bore a tale of survival.

In this vibrant yet volatile neighborhood, my early years unfolded with an appearance of normalcy, grounded in the warmth of family life. My father's laughter was amazing. He filled our modest apartment with a sense of security and love. My mother was strong. She always made sure that we were staying out of trouble, and she gave us the voice that we needed to survive living in the streets of Brooklyn. Together, they made the home feel warm. Then, one day, it wasn't so warm anymore.

When I was ten years old, my parents decided that they needed to split up, which now, as an adult, I know was for the best. Behind the warmth of living with both of my parents, there was also a lot of fighting. After having three kids, my parents grew apart. My mom asked my dad to move out, and he did just that.

Navigating that was interesting. Coming home from school and not seeing my dad was hard, but I sucked it up because, after all, in the streets of Brooklyn, having both mom and dad living at home was a rare occurrence. Just as I was getting the hang of things, my mom got a call. Orestes, my dad was in the hospital. He was throwing up blood, and he was not doing well.

That day, the word Cancer was introduced to me... I was ten. I had no idea what it meant, but I knew that my dad was sick and in the hospital. My dad was diagnosed with terminal cancer. We had no idea where it started, but he had lung, stomach, and colon cancer. We got a whole six months with him after his diagnosis.

The sudden loss of my father to cancer was like a storm that broke the fragile peace of our household. At just ten years old, the gravity of his absence was a burden too heavy to bear. The void he left was immensely affecting not just our family's emotional landscape but plunging us into financial turmoil.

My mother, already a figure of strength amid adversity, faced the daunting task of navigating the stormy waters of single parenthood. The challenges were overwhelming: grappling with her grief while trying to shield us from our own, struggling to make ends meet, and filling the emptiness left by my father's departure.

The impact of losing my father was profound, reshaping our existence. The occasional moments of joy we once shared were overshadowed by a constant undercurrent of struggle. My mother's resilience was our guiding light, yet the absence of my father's presence left a void that seemed overwhelming. This altered reality and laid the groundwork for my later battles with sadness, anxiety, and depression beneath the surface of a childhood overshadowed by loss and resilience.

The streets of Brooklyn, with their intricate tapestry of danger and community, became the backdrop against which my internal battles unfolded. Yet, it was also where I learned about strength, the importance of community, and the value of dreaming of a world beyond the immediate confines of my challenging reality.

My father's death was a turning point, plunging me into a depth of sadness and confusion that a child could barely comprehend. The loss brought about a profound sense of vulnerability and abandonment, emotions that would later manifest as anxiety and depression.

The neighborhood, with its symphony of sounds and whirl of activities, was both a playground and a battleground. My early encounters with violence—a fistfight breaking out in the park, the sharp report of gunfire disturbing the night—taught me the harsh realities of survival. I learned to navigate these streets with a mix of fear and fascination, understanding that to survive here, one must develop a thick skin and a quick reflex. These experiences, though traumatic, were also the crucible in which my resilience was forged.

Yet, amidst the chaos, there were havens of peace and imagination. "The Little Mermaid" became more than just a movie; it was an escape, a portal to a world where the grim realities of my existence did not confine dreams. Ariel's longing to explore beyond her world mirrored my own desires to find a place where the weight of grief and the sting of poverty did not exist. Singing "Part of Your World" at the top of my lungs, I could momentarily drown out the sound of my surroundings and the turmoil within my family.

Despite these brief respites, the shadow of mental health issues loomed large. My adolescence was marked by a pervasive sadness, a feeling of being perpetually adrift. The anxiety was like a constant hum in the background, sometimes escalating into a deafening roar that made concentration in school nearly impossible. Depression followed a shadow that dimmed the brightness of my teenage years. During these times, the disparity between my inner world and the facade I presented to the outside became most pronounced.

The stigma surrounding mental health in my community, coupled with the personal shame of admitting weakness, meant that these battles were often fought in silence. My few attempts to share my feelings were met with well-intentioned but ultimately dismissive advice to "toughen up" or "shake it off." It was a lonely fight that made the moments of joy and solace all the more precious.

In the midst of this struggle, there were glimmers of hope and resilience. My mother, despite the overwhelming burden of her own grief and the task of raising three children alone, was a pillar of strength. Her tough love, though often expressed through a prism of worry and exhaustion, was a constant reminder that we were not alone in our battles.

High school brought new challenges but also opportunities for growth. As my teenage years progressed, the lessons learned on the streets of Brooklyn and the coping mechanisms developed in the solitude of my struggles began to blend into a sense of identity. The resilience instilled by my upbringing, the empathy born from my internal battles, and the creativity encouraged by my escapes into imagination laid the groundwork for the person I was becoming.

Yet, the journey was far from over. The transition from adolescence to adulthood would bring new challenges, forcing me to confront my past traumas and embark on a path toward healing. It was a journey that would take me far from the streets of Brooklyn, literally and metaphorically, but ultimately lead me back to myself.

This period of my life, filled with darkness and light, taught me invaluable lessons about the complexity of human experience. It showed me that within each of us lies the capacity for immense suffering and incredible resilience. My childhood and adolescence, with all their trials and triumphs, were not just a time of struggle; they were a profound education in the depths of sorrow, the heights of joy, and the unbreakable spirit of survival.

At 23, my life took a crucial turn. I moved out, stepping into a new chapter that felt amazing. It wasn't long before I met the man who would become my husband. Our whirlwind romance led to marriage, and together, we embarked on an adventure that promised a fresh start, away from the echoes of my troubled past. This move to Canada was my "Little Mermaid" moment—my leap into a world I had longed for, a world where I believed I could leave the shadows behind and embrace the light of my very own happily ever after.

Arriving in Canada in September 2023 was like stepping through a portal to a different universe. The air was fresher, the streets quieter, and the sense of safety palpable. It was everything I had dreamt of and more. The initial months were filled with a sense of hope and exhilaration. I was finally living my dream, or so I thought.

The novelty began to wear off as autumn turned to winter, and the stark reality of starting over in a new country set in. It was during this period of adjustment that the first signs of trouble appeared. The memories and traumas I had naively thought I could outrun began to resurface, casting a shadow over my newfound happiness. It was a gradual realization that no matter how far I ran, my past was always just a step behind, waiting for a moment of vulnerability to catch up.

By April, the internal turmoil had reached a breaking point. One sunny afternoon, while driving home from volunteering at a women's program, a flood of memories from my childhood overwhelmed me. The voices of despair and self-doubt that I had worked so hard to silence began to scream inside my head, urging me to end my suffering once and for all. It was in that moment of sheer panic and confusion that I nearly steered my car into a ditch, convinced that there was no other escape from the pain.

Shaken by the experience, I realized I needed help. Desperately.

It was a humbling acknowledgment that my battles were not something I could face alone. The following days were a blur as I navigated the Canadian healthcare system, a daunting and unfamiliar process.

My first encounter with a mental health professional was a turning point. After a series of assessments and heartfelt conversations, I was diagnosed with Complex Post-Traumatic Stress Disorder (C-PTSD). The diagnosis was both a shock and a relief. For years, I had struggled to understand the depths of my sadness, anxiety, and despair, and now, finally, there was a name for it. It validated my experiences but also marked the beginning of a long and uncertain journey towards healing.

The diagnosis of C-PTSD was a critical turning point in my life. It was the moment when the weight of my past traumas, which had been silently accumulating like shadows, was finally brought into the light. The realization that my struggles had a name—and, more importantly, a path towards healing—was a profound relief. Yet, it also marked the beginning of the most challenging journey I had ever undertaken.

Recovery was not a straight line but a series of peaks and valleys, each with its own set of obstacles and victories. The first step was finding the right therapist, someone who specialized in EMDR (Eye Movement Desensitization and Reprocessing) therapy, a treatment recommended for individuals struggling with PTSD.

This therapy was unfamiliar and, frankly, intimidating at first. It required me to revisit some of the darkest moments of my childhood, to face the memories and emotions I had spent years trying to bury.

Each session was a battle in its own right. There were days when the progress seemed tangible, moments when I felt a shift within myself—a lightening of the burden I had carried for so long. Yet, there were also days when the sessions left me exhausted, emotionally spent, and doubting whether healing was truly possible. The memories that surfaced were often painful, a vivid reminder of the experiences that had shaped me in ways I was only beginning to understand.

Despite the challenges, I committed to the process. With my husband's unwavering support and my therapist's guidance, I began to notice subtle changes. The nightmares that had haunted my sleep became less frequent, the moments of panic and anxiety more manageable. It was a slow transformation, one that required patience, perseverance, and an immense amount of courage.

Recovery also meant learning to navigate the world in a new way. I had to relearn how to trust, not just in others but in myself. I had to build a new foundation of self-worth and identity, one not defined by my past traumas but by the strength and resilience I had shown in facing them.

This healing journey was not just about confronting the past; it was about shaping a future where I could thrive, not just survive.

As I reflect on the road to recovery, I am reminded of the complexity of the human spirit. Healing from C-PTSD has been the most challenging journey of my life, but it has also been the most rewarding. It has taught me that vulnerability is not a weakness but a strength, that seeking help is a step towards empowerment, and that healing is not only about moving past the pain but also about rediscovering joy, hope, and the possibility of a new beginning.

Now, years into my journey, I stand on firmer ground. The echoes of my past still linger, but they no longer define me. I have learned to embrace my story, with all its scars and beauty, as a testament to my resilience. And while the road ahead may still hold its share of challenges, I move forward with a heart full of gratitude, a mind armed with knowledge, and a spirit unbroken, ready to face whatever comes with courage and hope.

Starting on the journey of rebuilding my life post-therapy felt like standing at the edge of a huge, uncharted territory. The landscape of my existence, once marred by the scars of trauma, now lay open and ready for new foundations to be laid. Deliberate choices marked this phase of my life, each step taken with the awareness of the delicate balance I had begun to develop within myself. The process was not just about healing from the past but actively constructing a future where I could thrive, not merely survive.

Another significant step in my journey was starting a family. The decision to become a parent was filled with concerns and doubts. The fear that I might somehow pass on my traumas to my child, that I would not be capable of providing the stability and love they deserved, weighed heavily on me. Yet, with the support of my husband and the skills I had learned in therapy, I embraced this new chapter.

Parenthood brought its own set of challenges and joys. It forced me to confront aspects of my past that I had yet to fully reconcile, particularly around my family dynamics and my childhood experiences. Yet, it also offered a profound sense of healing. In striving to create a nurturing environment for my child, I found aspects of my own wounds beginning to mend. The experience was transformative, revealing reserves of strength and love I had not known I possessed.

Perhaps one of the most crucial elements in building my new life was the role of community. The isolation I had felt during my darkest periods had underscored the importance of connection and belonging. I found myself initially adrift in Canada, lacking the natural networks that come from a shared history and culture. Building these connections required effort and vulnerability, reaching out to neighbors, coworkers, and fellow parents, often stepping outside my comfort zone.

I also sought out communities that resonated with my experiences, joining groups focused on mental health, parenting, and professional development. These spaces offered not just support but opportunities for growth and contribution. They allowed me to share my story and listen to others, creating bonds forged through shared understanding and mutual respect.

The importance of these communities cannot be overstated. They provided a sense of belonging that had been missing from my life, a reminder that I was not alone in my experiences or my aspirations. They were spaces where my past did not define me but rather informed me how I could contribute to the world around me. Through these connections, I learned the true meaning of resilience, not as a solitary journey but as a collective endeavor supported by the strength and compassion of those around us.

Looking back on the journey of rebuilding my life, I am struck by the interplay of strength and vulnerability, of individual effort and community support. The road from the depths of despair to a place of stability and hope was long and filled with challenges. Yet, each step was a testament to the capacity for change and the human spirit's ability to overcome adversity and forge new paths.

The life I have built is not without its struggles. The shadow of mental health issues is a constant companion, requiring vigilance and care to manage. Yet, it is also a life filled with joy, purpose, and connection. It is a life that is deeply mine, shaped by my experiences but not defined by them.

In sharing this journey, my hope is to offer a light to others navigating their own paths of healing and growth. To show that while the road may be difficult, it is also dotted with moments of profound beauty and connection.

Building a new life post-therapy is not just about moving beyond trauma; it's about embracing the fullness of our human experience, with all its complexities and contradic-tions, and stepping into the world anew, resilient and whole.

As I reflect on my journey from the shadowed streets of

Brooklyn to the tranquility of my new life in Canada, it's clear that the path of healing and growth is not linear but a spiral, ever-evolving and circling back to lessons learned along the way.

This journey has been both a battle and a ballet, a negotiation between the scars of the past and the possibilities of the future. The transformation within me speaks to the resilience of the human spirit, the capacity to face darkness and choose light, to confront pain and choose healing.

The most profound lesson I've learned is that vulnerability is not a weakness but a source of strength. Opening up about my struggles with mental health was one of the hardest steps I've ever taken, but it was also the most liberating. It taught me the power of authenticity, of owning my story with all its imperfections, and the incredible strength that can be drawn from simply saying, "I need help." This vulnerability allowed me to connect with others on a deeper level, forging bonds of understanding and compassion that have become the bedrock of my recovery and growth.

Another invaluable lesson has been the understanding that healing is not a destination but a journey. There are no quick fixes for the wounds we carry, but every step forward, no matter how small, is a victory. It's a process that requires patience, kindness, and the courage to face ourselves fully, even when we'd rather turn away.

My experiences have taught me that growth often comes from the most unexpected places, and resilience is built not in the absence of struggle but through navigating it.

To those who are in the midst of their own battles, know that you are not alone. Your pain does not define you, nor does it diminish your worth. There is hope, even in the darkest moments, and strength within you that you may not yet realize.

The journey toward healing is grueling and often winding, but it is also filled with moments of profound beauty and connection. Reach out, share your story, and allow others to walk beside you. The path of recovery is one that is best traveled together.

Today, I stand in a place of gratitude and reflection, looking back on the journey that has shaped me into the person I am. My life is a testament to the fact that change is possible, that healing is attainable, and that every day brings a new opportunity for growth. My current status is one of continued evolution, a daily commitment to living authentically and pursuing a life filled with purpose and joy.

My dreams and aspirations are now focused on using my experiences to help others find their path to healing. Whether through advocacy, writing or simply being present for someone in need, my goal is to be a source of hope and encouragement.

The ongoing nature of healing and personal growth reminds me that there is always more to learn, more to explore, and more ways to contribute to the world around me.

My journey from the depths of despair to a place of healing and growth is a story I share with the hope that it might light the way for others. It's a reminder that even in our darkest moments, we possess the power to rewrite our narratives, to choose resilience, and to emerge stronger, ready to face the world with courage and hope. The path is not easy, but it is worth every step.

"Every failure is a gift. Every pain is an opportunity."
Maxime Lagacé

10

FINDING STRENGTH THROUGH LIFE'S CHALLENGES: HOW AN UNEXPECTED JOURNEY LED TO RESILIENCE, EMPOWERMENT, AND A NEW ME

MELODIE DEWSBURY

"Every time I let someone take advantage of me, the more I allow my self-respect to be chiselled away."
Lightbulb Moments

My mid-life crisis started when I was 32, and I found naked photos of another woman on my husband's phone. Before you judge me, I had never looked at his phone before without his knowledge. But something told me that morning that I needed to and that what I would find would answer many questions.

This story was originally going to be based on the situation I found myself in after that morning, how I navigated through my husband's year-long affair, as well as the separation and divorce that followed.

The day after International Women's Day, while I was straightening my hair, I started singing, "Anything you can do, I can do better, I can do anything better than you," which had been stuck in my head all morning. Strange, since I hadn't thought of that song in years. My grandma sang it to me every Saturday morning after a sleepover while she made me pancakes and bacon. It wasn't just because of her love of Annie Oakley or because she was always singing when she made breakfast, but also because she was trying to instill a core belief that I might carry with me throughout my life.

I messaged my grandma to tell her about this earworm (a song you can't get out of your head), and she sent me a beautiful text back about how much she loves me, how she had recently been following my social media posts from the new company I work for (a female-led and all-female business consulting agency), and how proud she is of me. It was her way of saying, "I told you so!"

My grandmother has always been a pseudo-parental figure in my life. I've often gone to her for advice or to share my accomplishments. I often hear her voice in my head when I make decisions.

I sat there for a minute or two with a smile on my face, and then a lightbulb came over my head. "Melodie, THIS is what you need to write about in this chapter."

While I was originally going to sit down and summarize all the juicy details of the affair, the separation, and how I moved on with my life despite the PTSD that manifested itself from that situation, it was this conversation with my grandmother that made it clear to me I wouldn't be where I am today without the women in my life (literally and figuratively).

It's about what I learned from this traumatic period of my life and how it's shaped me to be who I am today. It's also about the women who played a pivotal role in my recovery because the women who surrounded me on this journey were Women Like Me.

If you're lucky, you grow up surrounded by people who are there to help mold you into who you're meant to be, guide you along the way, and instill values that carry you throughout your life. Hopefully, their influence means you accomplish a lot in your lifetime.

I am extremely lucky in this sense, as my parents were divorced and remarried to great people, so I had multiple strong female role models in my life. With strong role models come strong beliefs that you might adopt. And I did.

Beliefs such as work hard, be kind, help others. Go to school to get a good job. Start a family, move up in your career, save for retirement. Marriage is a life-long commitment, a one-time shot, no matter what comes your way.

The Morning That Changed Everything

I met my ex-husband, finished my degree, started my career in education, experimented with entrepreneurship, and we got married. By the time I had turned 27, I had checked off a lot of boxes! Not bad, right?

From the outside in, I should have been happy, but I struggled with depression since my early 20s and wondered often what the hell was wrong with me. I thought the reason for this depression was chemical or genetic since it ran in the family (but I later found out it was not that at all).

I had accomplished a lot, but deep down, I wasn't really doing what lit me up. In a way, I felt stuck on a path that didn't belong to me. I enjoyed teaching, but it wasn't my dream. It was a career choice I followed because I was "good" at it, and I didn't know what else to do with my life. Following other people's dreams will only make you so happy (hindsight is always twenty-twenty).

I was married to a great guy. To me, we had a normal marriage. We rarely fought, we compromised when needed, and supported each other in our careers and personal lives. He was fairly supportive of all my little hobbies and crazy ideas that started my entrepreneurial career. We even had some big plans for our life. But they were "our" plans and not "my plans" because they involved us both becoming leaders in our industry and as I said, I had never taken a hard look at what I wanted to do with my life. It seemed like a good path, so I went along with it.

About four years into our marriage, he started acting differently and very much out of character. My gut told me something wasn't right. He became increasingly agitated with me, picked fights with me, and didn't want to even be around me.

One weeknight, he was out until almost two am, claiming he was running errands. There was "so much traffic" at this time of night, which is why he was late. Needless to say, I wasn't buying it. I felt like my gut was screaming at me, "This is not right."

That morning, while he was in the shower and getting ready for work, I unlocked his phone, and right there on the screen was a photo of a naked woman. I didn't even have to open any apps, as this was the last thing he looked at on his phone.

I was shocked and confused to realize it was somebody I knew.

The details of that morning are a chapter in itself. Confronting him that I knew about his affair and having to tell my family (who loved him like a son/brother/grandson) were the two hardest things I had to do. The second hardest thing was deciding how to spend the rest of my day with this information. The world kept spinning somehow, like it didn't matter that my life had just turned upside down. My mother and sister dropped everything that day and drove over an hour to help me put one step in front of the other.

I was in extreme shock and could barely function (queue the PTSD). I could not reconcile that he could do this to us. Marriage, after all, was a serious promise, with vows and everything, and instantly everything was broken. I was completely shattered. How could someone who I knew so well have lived a secret life? How could someone who supposedly loved me SO much do something like this? How could I not know?

Nothing made sense to me, except that it must have been something I had done. It must have been those years I was depressed that drove him away. I wasn't good enough to be his wife.

To this day, I struggle internally, saying out loud that I have PTSD. The severity of the trauma I went through pales in comparison to the trauma that so many other women experience daily. I was shocked when my counsellor diagnosed me with PTSD a year later and felt guilty right away. Since then, I've learned that someone's trauma isn't more "significant" than another person's trauma. There's Big T Trauma and Little T Trauma; even if someone has gone through a deeply distressing experience, that's enough to be diagnosed.

Conversations with Strong Women

In the coming days, I sought the advice of two very strong women I knew who had both survived their husbands' affairs. At this point, I was fully committed to making my marriage work (early on, not knowing all of the details of the affair and others that surfaced). But I needed to know what I would be up against, so I met with both women separately and asked for their advice.

My one friend decided to stay and repair the damage. On the outside, it appeared that they had resolved all their issues and were doing great but she shared with me that at times she regretted that decision and that she had a lot of guilt, shame, and paranoia.

My other friend immediately left after finding out about her husband's affair. She started over as a single mom and rebuilt herself in the process.

Their advice to me was that there was no easy way out. I remember discussing these conversations with a close family member who added, "There is no right or wrong answer, whatever you choose."

For a couple of weeks following the naked photo incident, my ex-husband couch-surfed while I stayed at our house. He came and went, we discussed the future of our relationship (should we work on it, what would this look like, etc.) and he tried to get back into my good graces so he could move back in. Again, I was fully willing to work on our marriage.

A few days later, I let him move back into the basement (so he'd at least have a room instead of someone's couch – looking back, this was too kind) and found out he was still seeing the woman he cheated on me with. What was the point of our conversations about trying to move forward? What a waste.

My aha moment (the first of many to come) came after a conversation with a girlfriend after learning this news. She reminded me that every time I let someone take advantage of me, the more I allow my self-respect to be chiselled away.

I'm going to repeat that again because it is the most pivotal moment in my entire life to date and that single sentence changed the entire course of my life.

Every time I let someone take advantage of me, the more I allow my self-respect to be chiselled away. Hearing that was like having someone hit me in the head with a brick. I was not raised that way.

It was all of a sudden very clear to me he was not interested in changing his behaviour and he would continue to hurt me as long as I let him.

Finding Solace in Solitude

Over the next few months, I re-established myself as a single woman, and I truly felt as if I had an army of women supporting me. What kept me going were weekend visits, girls' nights, secret chats in the library book room at lunch, and gifts from female mentors and friends that inspired me immensely.

I learned to live on my own again, finding new hobbies to fill the long days (oh my God, where they ever long) and learning to enjoy being in my own company. In hindsight, I may have learned to do that too well because I now love to sit in a quiet house all by myself, and living with others sometimes feels very hard.

Somehow, my depression was gone, but I struggled medically with a physiological disorder I'd been dealing with since I was a kid. Teaching became increasingly difficult, and while I started to feel pretty great mentally, I wasn't sure I could keep up physically.

The second aha moment in this story came from me: once again, my intuition was screaming at me, much louder than the first time I heard it that morning in our bedroom before my world was turned upside down. I knew something had to change, but I was in control this time. I could do whatever I wanted to do. Nobody was there to tell me no or to convince me otherwise. Despite not knowing if it would work out, I had to trust myself. What I was doing wasn't making me happy, and I desperately wanted to be happy and in control of my life.

I was about to embark on a new journey: entrepreneurship.

This is not the part of the story where I tell you everything turned out perfectly. In fact, I call this next phase of my life my second (and third) rock-bottom moment.

For two years, I continued to work and grow my business on the side. In 2019, when I finally decided to quit teaching, I had approximately five side hustles going at one time. It was a lot, but it worked—until six months later, when we were all thrown a curveball and we were all introduced to Covid-19.

Diamonds Are Formed Under Pressure

Just before the pandemic happened, I was hit with a lawsuit. While my ex and I had been sharing the dog like a divorced child every week, my dog's health was suffering. For a woman who doesn't have any kids of her own, this dog was (still is) my baby, and I just couldn't let his health deteriorate anymore. I decided, for his sake, not to share him anymore. I really hoped my ex would understand, seeing the need to put the dog's health first. Maybe, just maybe, after everything that happened between us and after so much lying and betrayal, he'd have some compassion for me and leave it alone. I took a chance, legally, since I was in breach of our separation agreement, but it bit me in the ass.

I was already struggling before the pandemic hit, but with this new situation came a whole slew of other financial issues (as so many others around the world experienced too).

In a phase of my life where a lot of things were up in the air, there were some I was certain about: I was going to do everything in my power to keep my dog, I had family that loved and supported me (even if they thought I was crazy for leaving teaching and potentially needing to sell my house), and I would be okay wherever I ended up because I had my health, puppy, family, and friends. At the end of the day, this was all that mattered to me.

This was a really scary time in my life. I didn't have a job, I owed a lot of money in legal fees, and I was scared I was going to lose my baby.

I ended up paying tens of thousands of dollars to keep my dog. I didn't know if I'd have to sell my house, if the pandemic would ever end and I'd make money again, or how I was going to pay off all this new debt.

Reflecting on this year of my life, I have to give myself some credit. I did everything in my power to stay true to my beliefs, and I was the embodiment of resilience. I drew on my experiences and education and created income for myself in what seemed to be a time when everyone was struggling.

I tutored online, created logos and handmade gifts for people, rented out a room in my townhouse, and hustled in every way I could. I knew I had to keep going because nobody was coming to rescue me.

Footnote: my parents, grandparents, aunts, and uncles tried desperately to come up with solutions for me to keep my house, and this is exactly how I was able to stay in the home that provided me safety, solace, and a place to grow. I am forever grateful to them for supporting me like they did. Not everyone is as lucky as I was.

I continued to immerse myself in personal development courses and actively worked on myself. It wasn't long before I realized that I wasn't a victim—every time I hit rock bottom, I was being given a new lesson, taught to get comfortable with the uncomfortable.

I learned that limiting beliefs can be overcome and that negative voices in my head don't have to narrate my life in the future. Just because I think something doesn't make it true. Being alone suddenly hit me differently. I started to love my solitude.

It's said that success comes by putting one foot in front of the other and slowly making your way to the finish line, even if it takes baby steps. This is an accurate description of the next few years of my life.

Mid-pandemic, I started a confidence and empowerment coaching business. It quickly took off and eventually morphed into digital marketing and social media coaching as so many people moved their businesses into the online realm.

This became my main source of income for a few years, and this might have been the most fulfilling time of my life. Not because I was making a lot of money (because I wasn't) but because I was stepping into a version of myself I didn't know existed and creating a path for myself I never imagined I'd be able to create.

The Power of Female Support

Reading the text message from my grandmother this morning summed up this whole chapter for me. I've had strong female role models my whole life to guide, support, push, and challenge me. And occasionally root for me when I have the craziest ideas (like selling my house to travel the world with my dog mid-pandemic and returning to live in a tiny home somewhere – I didn't actually do this, but I came close!).

My grandmother's text message made me realize that my story of scandal, divorce, PTSD, shame, guilt, and re-entering the dating world in my mid-30s wasn't the juicy story I wanted to tell in this book, but more so about the women that helped me get to where I am today.

It's no coincidence that this revelation came the day after International Women's Day and that I'm writing this chapter in a book titled "Women Like Me." The universe was waiting for me to make these connections and inspired me to start writing from this perspective. The universe always has a way of reminding me what's important when I'm in the thick of it.

I think about the women in my life now...I have many female friends and I cherish deep one-on-one connections with my girlfriends.

I don't consider myself a girly girl, and maybe I'm more of a tomboy. I like building things with power tools, I'll wear plaid instead of a skirt, and I like to learn how to do things that men typically do (because "anything you can do, I can do better").

While I'm still an entrepreneur at heart, I eventually took a break from my business and am now a marketing manager for another female entrepreneur and all-female company, a position I could not have been offered without the last several years of trial-and-error, going it alone, and making a name for myself.

The story I originally wanted to tell was how I'd been wronged and how I moved from being the victim to the hero of my own story. While that's still true, the following is also true: Life changes. Sometimes, you gotta go with the flow.

I started off by following my dreams and shifted the meaning of success and what those dreams looked like as I went, and that's okay. It's alright to try something (like entrepreneurship) and decide it might not be right for you or not right for you at this time of your life. There aren't any rulebooks here.

I'm so happy to be in a serious relationship and start a new chapter after my divorce.

I'm learning to stand up for myself in a way I never have before in my relationships, friendships, family dynamics, and career.

At the end of the day, being a human (and a woman at that) is a wild ride, and if you can create a life you are proud of and all that encompasses, then that's all that matters.

"Change happens when the pain of staying the same is greater than the pain of change."
Tony Robbins

11

LOVE'S MANIFESTATION: LETTING LOVE IN AND TEARING DOWN WALLS

JULIE FAIRHURST

"So, I love you because the entire universe
conspired to help me find you."
Paulo Coelho

Marriage at the tender age of 17, three sons by 24, and a reckless husband who seemed to be on a constant path of self-destruction. This was the life I found myself in, where I was our family's financial pillar. I had to be the responsible one!

The constant battles and the endless attempts to steer my husband away from his foolish decisions eventually led to the disintegration of our marriage. Thus began my journey as a single mother, a journey that would span the next 24 years.

Over the years, I had my fair share of relationships. But none of the men seemed like the marrying type. Even when proposals came my way, I turned them down, choosing to move on instead. Looking back, it's intriguing to see the pattern of men I attracted. Many bore an uncanny resemblance to my ex-husband - selfish, content with me taking charge, making decisions, and footing the bills.

I recognized this pattern and understood its roots, but changing it or making it stop was a challenge. None of these men were outright mean or nasty, but there was something off, something I couldn't quite put my finger on.

My tendency to give without expecting much in return was a product of my childhood experiences. My stepfather and mother never missed an opportunity to remind me of their generosity, contrasting it sharply with my father's lack of involvement. These memories built a wall around me, a barrier so high that no one seemed capable of scaling it. I made a resolution to take care of myself and never allow anyone to hold anything over me again.

The conflicting behaviors of my caregivers shaped my perspective on independence and self-reliance. I grew up believing in the importance of not being indebted to men. This belief influenced my approach to relationships and interactions throughout my life, leading me to prioritize independence and emotional self-reliance above all else.

Strangely, I didn't mind this dynamic; in fact, I preferred it. It ensured that I wouldn't feel indebted to any man.

One memorable dating experience involved a man who wanted to shower me with expensive gifts. But instead of feeling elated, I was overwhelmed with anxiety when he took me to a high-end jewelry store and expressed his desire to buy me a necklace.

I felt an urgent need to escape, to flee from the lavish store and the pressure of any obligations. Refusing to accept anything from him, I ended the relationship abruptly.

I would deliberately date men who seemed, or so I thought, to be different from the rest, but each time, I found myself in the same pattern. I started to question whether I truly felt deserving of someone caring for me.

My childhood was far from ideal. I grew up in a chaotic household filled with domestic violence and constant partying. There was never any sense of security from the adults around me.

Living in that environment likely led me to build a protective wall around myself, believing that if anything good was going to happen, I had to make it happen on my own. I didn't receive much help from others except for a few supportive girlfriends who were there for me when I hit rock bottom. Apart from them, I felt like I was completely on my own.

After going through numerous relationships, I finally met the perfect man for me - someone who needed care and support, which suited me just fine. He was a refugee from Iraq with no family here in the country. However, he had eight brothers and sisters back in Baghdad, not to mention nieces and nephews. Despite his challenging circumstances, he was a beacon of resilience and strength.

In a decade-long relationship, I found myself in a draining cycle of dependency. My partner, struggling with English, relied heavily on me for everything - from filling out forms to making phone calls and footing all the bills. Despite efforts to learn, his inability to read or write English only amplified this reliance.

As I reflect, I realize that I was partly to blame. I had chosen him, and he fit perfectly into my established pattern.

The breaking point came after a long day at work. Exhausted and seeking support, I was met with his own fatigue, which, as far as he was concerned, was more important than mine. That was when I lost my temper, demanding to know what more I could do to improve his life!

I knew deep down that I would never marry him. That moment was my turning point. I decided then and there that enough was enough - no more men for me. The end of this ten-year relationship brought with it a sense of relief. I had always been the one giving, often to my own disadvantage. For a decade, I had shouldered the burden of bills, holidays, and even financial support for my partner's family in the Middle East.

When it finally ended, a sense of freedom washed over me. The thought kept echoing in my mind: no more men, ever. Each time I allowed myself to trust someone, I ended up disappointed. I couldn't deny it any longer - it was my fault. I was the common denominator in all those failed relationships. I show all of them how to treat me. I permitted the toxicity, I enabled it, and I somehow managed to attract it into my life. I understood why this was happening and knew it was time for a change.

At first, the idea of staying single for good didn't seem all that bad. But deep down, I knew that wasn't the answer. The journey to freedom was not about avoiding relationships but about breaking free from the cycle of dependency and toxicity that had characterized my past ones.

It's easy to point fingers when relationships go sour. But the truth is, it takes two to tango. If you find yourself stuck in a cycle of unhealthy relationships, it's crucial to take a good, hard look in the mirror and acknowledge your own role in it all. You're a part of that dynamic, too, whether you realize it or not, and accepting responsibility is the first step toward positive change.

Maybe your contribution lies in the choices you make when selecting partners for reasons only you understand. But the good news is you have the power to change that pattern. It requires introspection and a willingness to focus on yourself and your own growth. When you're willing to do that, incredible things can happen.

And for me, it did.

My girlfriends practically had to drag me kicking and screaming back into the dating scene. I was feeling pretty uninspired about the whole idea and wasn't enthusiastic about giving it another shot. But eventually, I caved and decided to dip my toes back in the water by joining a dating site called "Match."

There were plenty of intriguing people on the site, and I went on a few coffee dates. But each time, I could tell right away that it wasn't going to work out. I was determined not to fall back into my old patterns, and I was confident that I wouldn't. After all, I had put in the work on myself and armed myself with all the newfound knowledge I had acquired.

Eventually, I was messaged by a man who tried a few times to set up a time for us to meet, but it wouldn't work out. This went on for about a month or more. Finally, we set a time that worked for both of us, and we decided to meet at a restaurant for a drink and appetizers.

We decided on a spot to meet, and I got there first. I watched for him coming up the street, and then there he was in the crosswalk, walking towards me. Well, it was the strangest thing. My brain said, "Oh, there you are," like I had been looking for him, and suddenly, there he was.

It was an odd start to our encounter. As he approached me, I found myself leaning in to kiss his cheek - a strange gesture given our unfamiliarity. Yet, there was an inexplicable sense of familiarity, as if we had known each other for years.

We found ourselves at a small table outside an Italian restaurant, the ocean view from our seats providing a picturesque backdrop to our meeting. The date was June 3, 2011, and the evening was bathed in glorious sunshine.

As our conversation unfolded, I felt a sudden surge of intuition. It was as if my psychic abilities suddenly kicked in, and I knew things. I casually asked him where he had parked. His response was prompt, "I parked down at my dad's place; he lives just down the street." Almost instinctively, I found myself asking, "Is that the burgundy house with the black roof?" I had singled out that one among the numerous houses lining the street.

His puzzled look confirmed my guess. "Yes, that's his house," he said. He must have thought I was a bit off my rocker when I continued, "I've been to that house before." On a whim, I asked if he had a brother named Craig. His affirmative response was accompanied by a revelation, "He's my stepbrother." Suddenly, it all made sense. "I remember now! I sold his apartment, and I met your stepmom. I had to go there to pick up the keys!"

The surprises didn't end there. Later in our conversation, he mentioned his plans to attend his daughter's baseball game the following day. Upon hearing the name of the park, I couldn't help but exclaim, "Oh, my niece plays ball there." His curiosity piqued, and he asked for my niece's name. His reaction upon hearing it was priceless. "Oh my god," he exclaimed, "that's my daughter's best friend! I know your sister and even met your mom at the ball field."

The situation was nothing short of surreal. The connections were uncanny, almost as if the universe had conspired to bring us together.

As the evening wore on, he opened up about his personal life, sharing details about his impending divorce and past relationships. A familiar name rang in my ears when he mentioned his ex-wife's name. It was another unexpected connection, another piece of the puzzle falling into place.

As our conversation deepened, he began to share more about his life. The impending divorce, the past relationships, and the intricate details of his personal journey.

In a moment of curiosity, I asked for his ex-wife's name. Upon hearing it, a spark of recognition ignited in my mind. Almost involuntarily, I found myself asking, "Does she have a sister named Christine?" His eyes widened in surprise as he confirmed, "Yes, that's her sister!" Unable to contain my excitement, I exclaimed, "I sold her house!" It was a revelation that left us both stunned. I knew his nephew and brother-in-law, too.

They had moved out of the area while I was in the process of selling the house. He had even shown up to clean out a shed for them before the new buyer moved in. The connections felt almost otherworldly. We marveled at how we had never crossed paths despite interacting with each other's family members multiple times.

Later, we discovered another bizarre coincidence. When his parents sold their home, they listed it with a friend of mine. I had gone on an office tour of the house, and he had been there too. Strangely enough, neither of us remembered meeting each other. This raised a question in our minds:

Were all these coincidences just random chance, or was there something more at play? Were we meant to be together?

As fate would have it, we were destined to be together. On December 12, 2012, we exchanged vows and merged our families. His three children and my three became a family of six.

Years have passed since then, and now we have married children and seven grandchildren, with an eighth on the way. This tale of serendipity reminds us that sometimes, life's most beautiful stories are written by chance.

Our relationship is a testament to the power of mutual respect and understanding. Over the years, we've navigated through life's ups and downs, disagreements, and moments of tension, yet we've never succumbed to a full-blown fight. We've always found ourselves on the same page, supporting each other through thick and thin.

Recently, an interesting incident took place during a dinner outing with five other couples. My husband was the only one (man) who paid the bill, while the rest of the husbands let their wives handle it. There's nothing inherently wrong with this, but it prompted a moment of self-realization for me. I decided to take a stand and refused to pay, not out of defiance but from a place of self-worth. I believe I deserve to be treated, and it brings me joy.

Our upbringing shapes us; sometimes, it's not a pleasant or healthy experience. However, it's up to us to take charge and make things better in our lives. Improvement doesn't just happen magically; it requires conscious effort and deliberate action. We need to wake up to our patterns and take responsibility for the direction our lives are heading.

It's crucial to understand that even if our circumstances aren't our fault, blaming others, even if they deserve it, won't lead us down a positive path. Instead, we should focus on what we want, how we want to be treated, and the kind of life we envision for ourselves. Once we've set our sights on our dreams, we need to hold onto them tightly and refuse to let go, no matter what challenges come our way.

Trust me, the universe has a way of bringing us exactly what we need and desire, and it'll be nothing short of spectacular. So, let's embrace the journey of self-improvement and mutual respect in our relationships and watch as life unfolds in the most beautiful ways.

"There is a saying in Tibetan, 'Tragedy should be utilized as a source of strength'. No matter what sort of difficulties, how painful experience is, if we lose our hope, that's our real disaster."
Dalai Lama

MEET THE AUTHORS

LOIS A UNGER

I WILL WAIT

CREATE YOUR OWN UNIQUE VISION TO EMERGE AS A QUEEN

Growing up on a small hobby farm instilled true values and an honest way of life. This paved the way as Lois navigated her road map through the years.

Owning a camera from a young age brought creativity to seize the moments and reflect. The arts genre for Lois included writing, photography, theatre, and how to embrace her aspirations.

Today, Lois calls herself a photo artist as she prints her images on select items for shops to display.

Modeling and acting have led her to rewrite her life story with much joy and empowerment.

Lois loves to create opportunities that benefit her wellness on all levels. Writing is a way for her to elevate her life and inspire others from her experiences. Lois uses words as a force to find the missing pieces and let her radiant self shine.

Every day, she strives to become a better fabuLOIS.

If you would like to contact Lois, you can do so below.

FACEBOOK: LOUUNGER

https://www.facebook.com/red.hen.98

INSTAGRAM: FABULOIS.05

https://www.instagram.com/fabulois.05/

TERRI-LYNN CATHERINE

EMBRACING MY WISE WOMAN

MY PATH TO SPIRITUAL SEEKING

Terri-Lynne has been a seeker of spirit her entire life. For 30 years, she has studied theology and metaphysics informally and formally. She is a healer and earth lover and practices her faith in an eclectic assortment of ways.

Mostly steeped in Celtic, Wiccan, and Native traditions, as well as the Christ Consciousness movement. She blends science and spirituality with deep leanings into the Earth sciences.

Terri-Lynne has led a very interesting life, to say the least; she likes to say, "Each decade seems like a new life path." She has been a successful entrepreneur, helping to start a multi-million-dollar salmon business back in the 90s after being a commercial fishing woman for nine years. Even through sea sickness Terri-Lynne carried on her duties out at sea and in the Fraser River.

At the close of the century and into the new millennium, she organized events in her hometown of Fort Langley, B.C., her first being the Beltane Bash held at the beginning of May, and then later, The Goddess Faire held at Autumn Equinox in September. She put on these festivals for six and seven years.

She also opened a metaphysical collective called Mystical Moments in Fort Langley in the year 2000. She studied Shamanism for many years, learning the ways of the Lakota mixed with Wicca, and became quite a prolific healer. She has studied various healing modalities over the years and is a writer and artist.

Terri-Lynne currently holds healing circles, does guided meditations, and is writing her memoir. She is a happy mother, grandmother, sister, and friend.

Terri-Lynne has been an Addiction Counselor and Recovery Coach for the last decade. She has shifted this work into working with youth at risk in Abbotsford, B.C. She enjoys being a part of and making a difference in these kids' lives. Terri-Lynne is also a Recovery Coach and is in her 15th year of sobriety.

Her current business is Terra Life Counselling Services, where she does Spiritual Counselling for those in need.

If you would like to reach out to Terri-Lynn, you can do so below.

EMAIL: terrischack@gmail.com

WENDY BERGEN

RECLAIM YOUR POWER

SO YOU CAN BE UNSTOPPABLE

Wendy supports women when facing adversity to Reclaim Their Power bringing them more clarity, confidence, and joy. She shares her 40 years of experience being a successful entrepreneur while raising two children who are now adults.

She is an International Renowned Transformational Solution Coach, Author, Motivational Speaker, and Podcaster https://thrivingatsixty.com

Wendy is also a Certified Reclaim Your Power (RYP) Workshop Leader, Transformational Coach - transforming your perception of yourself and others one conversation at a time.

Wendy learned early on to be an independent self-starter. Growing up in the foster system and experiencing violence in the home gave her a strong determination to create and build a better life for herself. She moved out at the age of 15 and put herself through high school, college, and university while holding down three jobs. Since then, she has started and sold six successful businesses. She is also the mother of two wonderful daughters and is delighted to be a grandmother!

Over the past 40 years, she has extensively researched and participated in transformational work. The results have been amazing. The combined result of her life experience and the changes she has been able to make by doing this work led her to become a transformational solution coach and speaker. She has a particular passion for making a difference for people who are starting over, whether it be relationship or work related. She has successfully coached thousands of people and delivered numerous presentations to business groups, associations, youth organizations, and others.

Wendy's commitment to your transformation is for you to be unstoppable; if she can do it so, can you! She believes that by transforming limiting beliefs, you can have clarity, freedom, and power in your life regardless of your circumstances. Her job as a coach is to help you to discover the barriers from the past that hold you back and teach you to let go of them. You will create new and effective ways of acting that inspire you, lighting you up to live the life of your dreams.

You can reach out to Wendy below...

GETTING UNSTUCK: 30 ways to turn YOUR limiting barriers into clarity, freedom and power

Amazon (Canada)

www.amazon.ca/GETTING-UNSTUCK-limiting-barriers-clarity-ebook/dp/B084X2BPHT

Amazon (United States)

www.amazon.com/GETTING-UNSTUCK-limiting-barriers-clarity-ebook/dp/B084X2BPHT

Instagram

https://www.instagram.com/thrivingatsixtyandbeyond/

Website

https://www.wendybergen.com/

DARLENE LONGO

THE STRONG ONE

ONE DIES, ONE SURVIVES

AND THE STORY IN BETWEEN

Darlene Longo's journey began in Toronto, Canada, where she was born and spent her formative years. Her current residence is in Trenton, Ontario, where she continues to cultivate her passion for the written word.

From a very young age, Darlene was captivated by the enchanting world of poetry and prose, a love affair that remains vibrant to this day.

Beyond her literary pursuits, Darlene is a multifaceted artist with a diverse palette of interests.

She engages in a variety of artistic endeavors, including working with textiles, painting, and sketching. One of her more unique ventures involves creating large, unconventional dream catchers intricately woven with lace and adorned with crystals.

These dream catchers are not just decorative items; Darlene crafts them with the intention of shifting energy, infusing them with a purpose beyond their aesthetic appeal.

Even when she is not busy writing, Darlene's creative spirit is seldom at rest as she continues to explore and experiment with different forms of artistic expression.

TRACEY GRAVES

OUR LOVE STORY

IN MEMORY OF CHRIS MASON

I'm a 59-year-old widow who used to love life after meeting my soulmate. I used to read a book every two days; now, my milestone is four in one year. After taking six months off from weight training, I went back to it and hard; I'm not competing, but it helps me mentally to get through the many days where I am broken.

I love to run but injured my knee during the pandemic. Technically, I am not supposed to run, but when I feel like I can, I do.

Pleasures: Watching hockey (Bruins vs Toronto) is always a fun rivalry for us. I love to play Golf, watch all the Chicago's on Wednesday night, Zumba and dancing. I am a huge advocate for animals; we were always very involved with Rescues.

Chris and I were very connected with the Partners in Mission Foodbank in Kingston (he was on the Board of Directors for nine years until he passed away). I continue his Legacy and Belief that "No One Should Ever Go Hungry" by hosting The Mason Golf Classic. We are in our 3rd year; in 2023 we raised over $17,500, 2024 here's hoping we can surpass that goal!

ASHLEY HILLARD

A STORY OF HEALTH, HEARTBREAK AND HEALING

FACING LIFE'S UNPREDICTABLE CHALLENGES, ONE OBSTACLE AT A TIME

Ashley lives on beautiful Vancouver Island with her husband, Jim, and their two fur babies, Rosie and Tabatha.

Ashley enjoys walks in the forest, relaxing time at the beach, metal detecting with Jim, and Geocaching.

She is looking forward to this new chapter in her life after being an E.C.E. (Early Childhood Educator) for 12 years.

After the fight of her life, she decided it was time for a change. Now embarking on a two-year Professional Counselor Diploma program at Rhodes Wellness College, Ashley is excited to become the very best counselor that she can be. She is learning that it's okay to have feelings and that they do matter.

Ashley loves to bake, cook, paint, draw, read, and write. She also loves spending time with her husband, close friends, and family.

CATHERINE CHAPMAN-KING

FINDING MY INNER LIGHT AGAIN

ECHOES OF LOVE

Catherine is a proud Toronto native with a unique journey that has shaped who she is today.

Catherine was adopted at the age of three alongside her biological brother. Growing up in a loving and nurturing home was a blessing, and it laid the foundation for who she is today.

Discovering her European and Indigenous heritage when she finally found her biological parents added richness and understanding to her identity. She embraced the diverse cultural background that flows through her veins.

Catherine's adoptive parents were the definition of pure love. They gave her a moral compass and so much more.

As a mother to five beautiful grown children and a proud Nan to nine grandchildren, the family has always been at the core of Catherine's being and the reason she lives.

Writing has been a lifelong passion, a creative outlet that allows her to express her thoughts, emotions, and experiences. Catherine's mission is to inspire, empower, and uplift others.

In addition to writing, she enjoys adventure and the great outdoors. Connecting with nature is vital to Catherine. She finds great pleasure in life's simple things and looks forward to each new waking day.

Catherine says, "It's another chance to make others smile and to create because life without art and creativity is just meh!"

LISA FAIRNEY

WALKING THE RAZOR'S EDGE

HOW PLACING ONE FOOT IN FRONT OF THE OTHER

GETS US THROUGH THE HARD MESSY TIMES

Lisa Fairney is a Mother, Grandmother, and what the people closest to her would call a modern-day Joan of Arc.

Lisa has devoted her life to serving her children, family, and community through personal and professional matters. She has a long-standing history of being an entrepreneur and starting service-based businesses.

Lisa has a heart of service and desires to see the people around her live in joy and feel cared about, whether it's taking care of children with special needs and chronic illness, caring for aging parents, or raising six kids and eight grandchildren, Lisa sees the gap in where people are most in need and fills it.

In 2018, her tenacity and persevering spirit of service led her to start a local business providing light therapy to people with neuropathy, arthritis, skin injuries, and more.

Her most notable achievement was being recognized by a local orthopedist, who sent her two patients who were close to needing leg amputations—and they were able to save both of their legs.

You can find more about Lisa and her work at:

Enlighten Me Therapy & Systems

https://enlightenmesystems.ca

LOUISA THIESSEN

THE COURAGE TO HEAL

A LIFE REBUILT ON RESILIENCE

Louisa Thiessen is a mom, wife, seasoned entrepreneur, C-PTSD survivor, and mental health advocate whose life story is a testament to the power of resilience and the human spirit's capacity to heal and thrive against all odds.

Born and raised in the vibrant yet challenging streets of Brooklyn, NY, Louisa navigated a childhood marked by trauma and adversity. Her early life, filled with challenges, shaped her into a fierce advocate for mental health awareness and women's empowerment.

After moving to Canada and overcoming her struggles through extensive therapy, Louisa founded Admin Virtuosa, a company dedicated to providing top-tier virtual administrative support to businesses while fostering a workplace that emphasizes mental health well-being.

Her work extends beyond business, touching lives through her advocacy, where she speaks openly about her journey with C-PTSD, aiming to destigmatize mental health issues and support others in their paths to recovery.

Louisa's life and work serve as a powerful testament to the idea that healing is within reach and that resilience can not only rebuild lives but can also inspire a community to rise together.

If you'd like to reach out to Louisa, you can do so below.

Instagram: https://www.instagram.com/iamlouisathiessen/

Facebook: https://www.facebook.com/LouisaThiessen/

Linkedin: https://www.linkedin.com/in/louisathiessen/

Email: Louisa@adminvirtuosa.com

MELODIE DEWSBURY

FINDING STRENGTH THROUGH LIFE'S CHALLENGES

HOW AN UNEXPECTED JOURNEY LED TO RESILIENCE,

EMPOWERMENT AND A NEW ME

In 2017, Melodie experienced a life-altering situation that led her on a new path of self-awareness, resilience, and independence.

In the years to come, she left her career in education to follow her dreams of entrepreneurship and making a name for herself. While she has recently taken on a leadership role in marketing, she is still an entrepreneur at heart.

Outside of working hours, you'll find Melodie crafting, painting, woodworking, gardening, or paddleboarding, where she finds both inspiration and tranquility.

Melodie now lives in the Fraser Valley with her partner, stepson, and fur-baby.

You can find Melodie here...

Instagram

@thisismelodiedee

Facebook

facebook.com/melodiedewsbury

Website

www.melodiedee.com

PART 2

WOMEN LIKE ME

12

DO YOU BELIEVE IN YOUR DREAMS?

During the spring of 2016, I questioned my life's purpose.

Despite a successful sales, marketing, and promotions career spanning over three decades, I had lost sight of my passion. Over the previous years, I had assisted more than three thousand satisfied clients, yet something was missing. I knew it was time for a change, but what direction should I take?

One evening, as I slept, I was awoken by a profoundly transformative vision in the form of a dream.

I recall being taken from where I was and led back. There was a bright light, and I said, "I don't want to go back; I want to stay here with you." I was told, "No, you have to go back; you're not finished yet."

I felt highly stressed and unhappy as I longed to remain where I was at that moment.

"But I don't know my purpose," I said. Someone responded, "You are your purpose." I recall experiencing anxiety and saying, "But I don't know what to do."

As I opened my eyes, a single word entered my mind: "Write!" Suddenly, I was fully awake.

Welcome to Women Like Me.

Julie Fairhurst

Founder of Women Like Me

13

A COMMUNITY OF WOMEN LIKE ME

If you do not already belong to the Women Like Me community, I encourage you to consider joining. It is a great place to find support and connect with other women. You can also participate in discussions, ask questions, and share resources.

Joining the Women Like Me Community is a great way to connect with women with similar experiences and learn from their successes and challenges. It can also be a fantastic way to find mentors and role models. So, if you are a woman looking for support, please consider joining the Women Like Me Community. You will not regret it!

The Women Like Me Community is a social network connecting women with similar interests, goals, and concerns. Whether you are a working professional or working at home and a stay-at-home mom, this community is for you.

The Women Like Me Community—Julie Fairhurst is a Facebook group of like-minded women who want to pay it forward and lift others up to promote healing in the world. They believe that by doing this, they can help create a kinder and more compassionate world.

The Women Like Me Community - Julie Fairhurst is a place where you can feel safe and supported. It is a place where you can be yourself and share your story. It is a place where you can find encouragement, inspiration, and connection.

Throughout the year, the community writes community books, such as the one you are reading now. All community members are encouraged to participate in the writing of the books. There is no cost to any of the writers who wish to share their wisdom in the community books. If you have always dreamed of being a published author, this is a wonderful community to start fulfilling your dream.

If you have been looking for a community where you can belong, this is it.

Don't wait, join today!

Women Like Me Community – Julie Fairhurst

https://www.facebook.com/groups/879482909307802

ABOUT JULIE FAIRHURST

A prolific author, visionary publisher, and an empowering writing coach helping women excel in life!

Julie Fairhurst is the Founder of the Women Like Me Book Program, part of the Julie Fairhurst Academy. She started the Women Like Me Project to help women tell their stories. Her unique storytelling programs allow her clients to share their message with the world. Julie has published 26 books to her credit and helped over 160 authors become published authors.

After spending 34 years as a sales, marketing, and promotional expert, Julie now helps women entrepreneurs build their influence and authority with their clients and customers to increase their revenue and profits. A Master Persuader Julie is an expert at understanding human behavior and what triggers people to make a purchase. She helps her clients develop marketing strategies that appeal to their target audience and provides coaching on closing the sale.

Julie is also a sought-after speaker, trainer, and prevention educator. She has delivered empowering workshops on safety issues to adolescents and adults and has presented to organizations such as the Vancouver Police Department, Justice Institute, University of British Columbia, Capilano College, Behavioral Society of British Columbia, Surrey Memorial Hospital, Teachers Association of North Vancouver, Shine Live, West Coast Woman's Show, Pink Stiletto Network, and more.

When Julie was young, her home life was chaotic and tumultuous. Her parents were constantly fighting, and she felt unsafe and unloved. As a result, she developed some bad habits and made poor decisions. As a teenager, she was headed down the wrong path, and it seemed like there was no hope for her.

But, somewhere deep inside, that little girl inside her showed up and reminded her that she wanted better for herself and her kids. Julie had no support from anyone, not a soul. She had to do it all on her own. She had no help from anyone, not a single person. She had to do everything by herself.

Many people say that you should never look back, but Julie does. Why? Because she wants to remember the journey that brought her to where she is today. And today, her life is very different.

Then, in 2019, Julie's beautiful 24-year-old niece died from a drug overdose on the streets of Vancouver, Canada. And that was the day she said enough! Her niece's death indirectly resulted from the generational beliefs and abuse that some of her siblings continue with their destructive lifestyles. So, when Julie says, "Enough is enough," she means it! Unfortunately, her story isn't unique.

When we don't face our issues, we pass on dysfunctional behaviors to future generations. This is what happened to her young niece. This is why she started the Women Like Me organization. When children grow up in toxic environments, they often develop behavioral issues that follow them into adulthood. This can lead to severe problems in their relationships, careers, and mental health. Julie's young niece was a victim of this.

Everyone has a story, and everyone's story matters. No matter what you've been through, you can improve your life. It's not always easy, but with determination and perseverance, anything is possible.

The first step is to believe in yourself. You have the power to create whatever future you want for yourself. The next step is to take action. You can't just sit and wait for good things to happen. You have to go out and make them happen.

And finally, you have to persevere. There will be setbacks, but that's no reason to give up. Keep going, and never give up on your dreams.

If you're willing to put in the work, you can change your life for the better. You have the power to do so. You have to believe in yourself and take steps to make it happen. So don't give up on yourself - you can do much more than you think. And when you're ready to start, Julie will be right here to help.

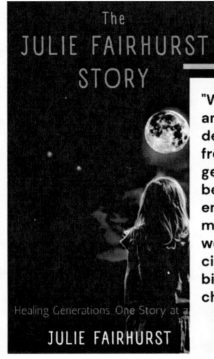

The
JULIE FAIRHURST
STORY

Healing Generations, One Story at a...

JULIE FAIRHURST

"While the road has been anything but smooth, the decision to break free from the cycle of generational trauma has been the most empowering chapter of my story, a reminder that we are not bound by the circumstances of our birth but defined by the choices we make."

Julie Fairhurst

REACH OUT TO JULIE

Email:
julie@changeyourpath.ca

Women Like Me Stories
www.womenlikemestories.com

YouTube – Julie Fairhurst Women Like Me Stores and in
Business https://www.youtube.com/channel/
UChFnLgiUC9mWnvp7jikKBw

Women Like Me on Facebook
https://www.facebook.com/StoryCoachJulieFairhurst

Julie Fairhurst Academy on Facebook
https://www.facebook.com/juliefairhurstcoaching

LinkedIn - Julie Fairhurst Certified Master Persuader
https://www.linkedin.com/in/salesstrategistjuliefairhurst/

Instagram – Women Like Me Stories
https://www.instagram.com/juliefairhurst_wlm_movement/

Facebook – Julie Fairhurst

https://www.facebook.com/julie.fairhurst.7

READ MORE FROM JULIE FAIRHURST
& THE WOMEN LIKE ME AUTHORS

All books are available on Amazon or the Women Like Me Stories website. If you can't find the book you are looking for, reach out to me, and I can help. Or if you would like an autographed copy, please email at julie@changeyourpath.ca

Women Like Me Book Series

- Women Like Me – A Celebration of Courage and Triumphs
- Women Like Me – Stories of Resilience and Courage
- Women Like Me – A Tribute to the Brave and Wise
- Women Like Me – Breaking Through the Silence
- Women Like Me – From Loss to Living
- Women Like Me – Healing and Acceptance
- Women Like Me – Reclaiming Our Power
- Women Like Me – Whispers of Warriors: Women Who Refused to Stay Broken
- Women Like Me – Embracing the Unseen – The Courage to Surrender
- Women Like Me - Transforming Pain Into Wisdom and Love

Women Like Me Community Book Series

- Women Like Me Community – Messages to My Younger Self
- Women Like Me Community – Sharing Words of Gratitude
- Women Like Me Community – Sharing What We Know to Be True
- Women Like Me Community – Journal for Self-Discovery
- Women Like Me Community – Sharing Life's Important Lessons
- Women Like Me Community – Having Better Relationships
- Women Like Me Community – Honoring the Women in Our Lives
- Women Like Me Community – Letters to Our Future Selves
- Women Like Me Community – The Warrior Within
- Women Like Me Community – Whisper's Within The Power of Women's Intuition

Women Like Me in Kenya

(100% of the profits go directly to these 26 Kenyan Authors. The Women Like Me Program covers all costs associated with producing and publishing the Kenya books)

- Women Like Me – Strong Women in Kenya
- Women Like Me – Through the Eyes of Kenyan Women
- Women Like Me – The Children of Kenya (Available June 2024)

Personal Growth, Writing, Business

- The Julie Fairhurst Story – Healing Generations, One Story at a Time
- From Idea to Bestseller – Writing for Self-Help Authors
- Positivity Makes All the Difference
- The Power of Penning – 20 Compelling Reasons Why Sharing Your Story Matters
- Elevate Your Business - Proven Strategies to Amplify Your Reach and Engagement
- Powerful Persuasion – Unlocking the Five Key Strategies for Business Success
- Transferring Enthusiasm - The Sales Book for Your Business Growth
- Agent Matchmaker: How to Find Your Real Estate Soulmate"

- Agent Etiquette – 14 Things You Didn't Learn in Real Estate School
- 7 Keys to Success – How to Become a Real Estate Badass
- 30 Days to Real Estate Action – Real Strategies & Real Connections
- Why Agents Quit the Business